LETTERS FROM THE SILK ROADS

Thinking at the Crossroads of Civilization

Eiji Hattori

Translated from Japanese by

Wallace Gray

University Press of America,® Inc.
Lanham · New York · Oxford

Copyright © 2000 by
University Press of America,® Inc.
4720 Boston Way
Lanham, Maryland 20706

12 Hid's Copse Rd.
Cumnor Hill, Oxford OX2 9JJ

Library of Congress Cataloging-in-Publication Data

Hattori, Eiji.
Letters from the silk roads : thinking at the crossroads
of civilization / Eiji Hattori ; translated from Japanese
by Wallace Gray.
p.   cm.
Includes index.
1.   East and West. 2. Silk Road. 3. Asia—Civilization.
4. Europe—Civilization. I. Gray, Wallace. II. Title.
CB251.H295   2000   950—dc21   00-062856 CIP

ISBN 0-7618-1828-6 (cloth: alk. ppr.)
ISBN 0-7618-1829-4 (pbk: alk. ppr.)

Contents

Preface

The "friend" to whom the letters in this book are addressed is you, the reader.

During the twenty-one years I served in Paris in the UNESCO headquarters, I've dealt with many projects. It was chiefly a matter of teamwork on three themes. These we may designate as:

- the common heritage of humanity
- intercultural exchange
- dialogue between science and culture

Because of these projects, before I realized it, I had visited 80 countries. Then, along with memories of the cultural assets and the beauties of nature, deep emotion welled up in my heart because of these many experiences with the people I have come across. Due to such experiences and memories and because of my location in the very international, intellectual city of Paris, my deep feeling began to transform itself gradually into an image—an image containing crucial features of the earth as seen from a satellite.

In addition to my work as a philosopher, I began to compose articles on comparative civilizations. The articles were published in the Japanese magazine *Risō* (ideals) and in other such magazines and journals. The essays concerned the theories and comparisons related to various cultures. When the opportunity to return to Tokyo arose, I collected these essays. I am offering this book to readers who along with me are thinking, "We would like to grasp human history" and who are willing to receive the book as an aid to this kind of thinking. Since the book is written from this point of view, I updated all essays previously published and added some new chapters. Some of these are my personal experiences in setting up and carrying out a project entitled, "An Integral Study of Silk Roads."

"Act as a thinker, and think as a man of action," Bergson once said. It seems that these words known from college days eventually engraved

themselves deeply on my heart and firmly guided my steps into an
international organization instead of a university.

The keen realization that has dawned on me while encountering
many people and joining with them in carrying out projects, and thus
walking the earth and viewing it from sky and sea, is the fact that up to
now education has warped knowledge. Cultural values are transmitted
in an extraordinarily distorted form. In world history, as described in
too many textbooks, there are many parts, and yet important parts are
missing. Why did such a thing happen? Also, why has the omission
been passed on to us without sound reflection? While thinking about
that, I noticed something. It is that modern textbooks still follow the
format of textbooks written in the 19th century, a period dominated by
science and colonialism. I have attempted in the seventh letter to
elucidate this issue of cultural warp.

However, science itself is not the thing that distorts history. History
is distorted by the spirit of an age nurtured by science. By means of the
most advanced theories of present-day science, a corrected perspective
on the world vision is arising. In this book, I didn't treat the
possibilities in the new encounters of cultural traditions and science,
possibilities that have been opened up by recent quantum physics and
biology. I would like to address such possibilities at another
opportunity.

The thing I want everyone to see is the image of earth revealed from
a space satellite. On the blue planet are floating the continents of
Eurasia and Africa. Boundaries cannot be seen there. . There are no
color codes or names attached to countries. Instead of that, from the
Sahel region of North Africa through Arabia and the Middle East, we
can see clearly a brown belt extending to the eastern part of China.
This is the true image of the earth.

The division of the map of human history into territories began in
the modern era. This territorial conception is related to the fact that
since the 18th century, Western Europe became increasingly powerful.
It inherited a political economy attached to land or areas. This
economy is called feudalism. Before that time the important things in
human history were points and lines that is, cities and routes. Lines
linking points became roads. The Silk Road is one of those.

This book takes the form of letters sent from various parts of the
world. I would like for everyone also to view the earth once again from
a satellite and to rethink the history of the people living there. When
you intently gaze at the brown belt which crosses Eurasia, you might

see in the midst of it tiny figures of nomads and caravans as well as monks and pilgrims coming and going. Furthermore, if you look at the blue space that occupies 70% of the surface of the earth, you may understand the role fulfilled by the sea in human history.

Translator's Preface to English Edition

Close consultation between the Japanese author and the American translator enabled the translation process to incarnate a key concept of the book. It is a "dialogue of civilizations." It is also a new edition as well as first translation, with additions such as footnotes, indexing, and new maps.

Reference works and historian Sidney Brown helped us establish a standard for the English spelling of proper names, especially for Eurasia.

Essential to the publication of this edition were: translation assistance from my Japanese students Rie Yanai, Noriko Kawabata, Rie Fujimaki, Kayoko Waki, and Soshi Kawabe; support from Reitaku Fund for the Promotion of Publication; research facilities at Southwestern College; Howard Buffum's proofreader's eye; Steve Ruggles' persistence and software expertise; guidance and finishing touches from the University Press of America. Ina Turner Gray acted as editor and publication facilitator.

Grateful acknowledgement is made: for reproduction in Letter 13 of the photograph of a Bodhisattva, courtesy of the temple of Horyuji in cooperation with Kodansha archives; for reproduction in Letter 11 of the photograph of Michelangelo's Florentine Pieta, courtesy of the Museum of the Opera del Duomo. Illustrations not otherwise designated were provided by the author.

Wallace Gray

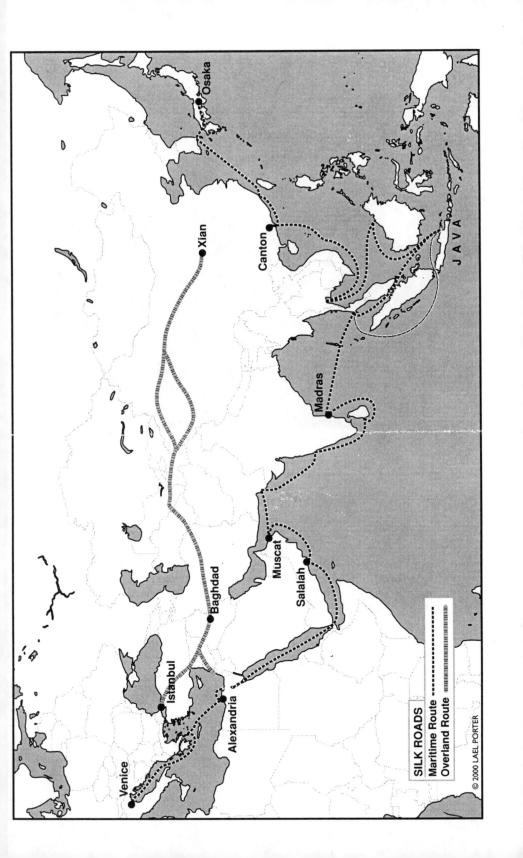

SILK ROADS
Maritime Route
Overland Route

© 2000 LAEL PORTER

Photo: Mohamed Mustafa

Fulk-al-Salamah (Ship of Peace)

UNESCO Maritime Expedition Itinerary

Venice, Italy
Athens, Greece
Kusadasi, Turkey
Alexandria, Egypt
Salalah, Oman
Muscat, Oman
Karachi, Pakistan
Goa, India
Colombo, Sri Lanka
Madras, India
Phuket, Thailand

Malacca, Malaysia
Surabaya, Indonesia
Bangkok, Thailand
Brunei
Manila, Philippines
Guangzhou (Canton), China
Quanzhou, China
Pusan, Republic of Korea
Hakata (Fukuoka), Japan
Osaka, Japan

Part I. Roads Connecting Civilizations

Letter 1

The Soul of the Silk Roads

Dear Friend,

"The silk roads, over land and sea, were above all the routes of dialogue between civilizations."

I expressed this thought in an opening statement I drafted for the UNESCO project "Integral Study of Silk Roads." However, since the original draft depended on intuition, it wasn't possible then as it is now to realize the full weight of the phrase "dialogue between civilizations." We could not then refute the statement, "The silk roads were primarily routes for war."

Nevertheless, this Silk Road project got support from the academic world and the member states of UNESCO. While we were moving to carry out this UNESCO enterprise as formally approved, I myself was coming to learn many things. Finally, not only were these words, "routes of dialogue," proving to be true, but also I came to feel the reality of how the past of the human race could shed light on the future of humanity. As reported by AFP's telex,[1] we had set sail "in search of time lost" (echoing the title of a novel by Marcel Proust[2]), the time when tolerance and respect for other cultures prevailed.

Our international team spent six years investigating these main routes. We held thirty seminars, involving more than 2,000 scholars, researchers, and journalists. All of this activity was the brainchild of one conversation.

---

[1] AFP = *Agence Française de Presse*
[2] The massive work is entitled, *A la recherche du temps perdu.* Published in English as *Remembrance of Things Past* (New York: Random House, 1934).

§

In the early summer of 1985, I was flying to Beijing from Pyongyang with my colleague, the Portuguese oceanographer Mario Ruivo. Because the small craft of the Chinese People's Republic would not fly over ocean water, we were taking a long detour to the north. Just when we passed over the Great Wall of China we looked down on a vastly eroded and barren earth. Suddenly a thought flitted through my mind, "In the midst of this vast expanse of space, there was once a road. It linked up with Persia."

Hattori: Mario, there were people in ancient times who, while risking death, travelled over this great barren land. They were seeking something . . . . Countless roads are hiding in these vast spaces. A certain Japanese poet said, "In front of me there is no road, but behind me a road stands," but 2,000 years ago there were travellers who actually had that kind of experience. Let us give careful consideration to our thought about human history. If there were no such travellers, most certainly history would have had a completely different form. By this road, East and West met each other. We may say, that on this foundation present human civilizations have been built. It's the Silk Road, indeed.

Mario Ruivo: Exactly! We can even say the 10,000 leagues of the Great Wall existed to protect caravan bands. The significance for human history of this interchange is something we should reflect on more deeply.

H: It is said that Japanese civilization also was born at the terminus of the Silk Road.

M: How about Portugal! My nation enters history at the very moment of its being connected by sea to other countries. Japan and my country are linked by sea.[3]

H: The sea route is also a silk road. In the West it is called the "Spice Route." Richthofen was the first to use this name of *Seidenstrasse* (Silk Road) in the 19th century. It is only a symbolic designation. It carried not only silk but also all kinds of goods, religions and thoughts. In this sense, the sea route is the same as the

---

[3] The reason for the maritime route is that Rome's enemy Parthia shut down the land route to Rome. Chinese silk was then shipped from the Malabar Coast in India to Alexandria via the Red Sea. Hence, the Roman name "Seres" (country of silk), a designation for both China and India.

Silk Road. In Japan the "Maritime Silk Road" is a phrase that has taken widespread root.

M: I agree that the sea route was also the Silk Road. For these and other reasons, the term *Silk Road* should be given a plural sense or spelling.

H: It is one network. The sea and land routes, then, are reciprocally or integrally interconnected with each other.

M: In UNESCO we are making an international compilation of human history, but until now no one has taken a close-up view of the Silk Road.

H: There you have it. In the early part of the 20th century, Sven Hedin, Aurel Stein, and Paul Pelliot investigated Central Asia as far as Dunhuang, the most famous Buddhist site in China.[4]   They acted as explorers for their own scientific research or the collection of materials for their national museums. It was, indeed, the time for pioneering. As for collaborative research with indigenous scholars in the field, this sort of thing had not entered anyone's mind.

M: Now even in so-called third-world countries, scholars of high professional quality have emerged. What is more, with the growing consciousness of cultural assets, we can feel the increasing distance between the time of such pioneers and our own time in that the scale of thinking has been enlarged to global proportions.   In the Intergovernmental Oceanographic Commission meetings I am dealing with, membership is not limited to developed countries only.

H: Mario, what then do you think of launching a study of silk roads by an international team in the name of UNESCO?

M: That's a terrific idea. It is the very mission of UNESCO. Roughly twenty countries must be involved with the Silk Road. We could send out teams of international scholars, experts on oasis routes,

---

[4] According to the article "Asia" in *Collier's Encyclopedia,* (1990 ed., III, 45), "The Swedish geographer, Sven Hedin, at first mainly interested in Mesopotamia and Persia, later became famous for his travels between 1893 and 1933 in Turkestan, Mongolia, and Tibet." Furthermore, "Sir Aurel Stein (1862—1943), was pre-eminent for archaeological discoveries which established the trade routes and cultural contacts between the Far East and the Mediterranean in ancient times." Paul Pelliot (1898—1945), one of the most famous sinologists in France, made three expeditions in Chinese Turkestan. The manuscript he brought back from Dunhuang Cave is preserved in Guimet Museum in Paris.

steppe routes, and sea routes. As they hold seminars, such activity will produce an interchange of opinions with indigenous scholars.

§

Even now I vividly recollect this airborne conversation. We were very excited about the possibilities it disclosed. Waiting for us when we arrived in Beijing was the chairman of the Chinese National Commission for UNESCO. As soon as we told him of the idea that had as yet not passed the germ stage, his immediate reaction was exceedingly good. Encouraged by that reaction, Mario, who returned to Paris a bit ahead of me, first communicated our idea orally to the Director General of UNESCO. Then, in order to get the criticisms of scholars from our own countries and others as well, I drew up a ten-page first draft in French beginning with the first sentence of this letter. The French scholar Vadime Elisseeff, the Japanese Takeo Kuwabara and Yasushi Inoue, the Pakistani Hassan Dani, the British Ms. Shirin Akinar were among the persons with whom I first consulted. Also, in every department of UNESCO, supporters appeared one after the other; in 1986 we created a preparatory committee (task force); then we invited about ten scholars living in Europe for preliminary study. In '87 the original form of the international consultative committee was completed. Professor Tadao Umesao, Director of the National Museum of Ethnology in Osaka, recommended two other Japanese: Kyuzo Kato, a specialist on the steppe route, and Takashi Wada from the newspaper *Asahi Shimbun*. I cannot forget the time in early '88 when I was requested to make a special announcement at London University on the occasion of a Central Asia Research Seminar. There, in addition to many English researchers, more than 30 participants from other countries had come together at their own expense. They listened eagerly to my announcement. I also recall an evening spent with Richard Fisher who made a "scout run" in a Land Rover on the steppe road that summer of '88. Subsequently I gave a live broadcast on BBC World News. My interview with the *Financial Times* appeared as a full-page article entitled, "Marco Polo, the Last Traveller on the Silk Road." All these events testify to the enthusiasm that prevailed at the launching of the project.

In '87 before Federico Mayor announced his candidacy for the post of Director General of UNESCO, he called me to express a high opinion of this Silk Road program. In Japan we received a swift promise of cooperation from the *Asahi Shimbun* newspaper group, the

National Museum of Ethnology, and the photographer Banri Namikawa. For the sea voyage we were able to receive from Sultan Qaboos of Oman the offer of the 11,000-ton royal yacht "Fulk al Salamah" (Ark of Peace). The origin of that offer goes back several years to when I happened to learn about the voyage of Tim Severin, a young British explorer. He had made a trip from Muscat to Hong Kong (the trip of Sindbad[5]) on board "Sohar," a reproduction of an ancient Arabian dhow. I procured a documentary movie of that voyage and viewed it with Ambassador Musa bin Jaffar of Oman. This was a decisive event. Ambassador Musa subsequently became a good friend who held a close connection with Mr. Malalah bin Habid, Undersecretary of the Ministry for Cultural Heritage of the Sultanate. He first made an offer, in accordance with my desire, of a three-masted sailing ship. However, because that ship was a training ship and did not have the capacity to lodge about 30 scholars, Oman offered us instead the sultan's royal ship Fulk al Salamah. Without this exceptional cooperation from both the Ambassador and Undersecretary, the 145-day voyage from Marco Polo's City of Venice to Port Naniwa[6] would not have become a fact. Our ship visited sixteen countries and twenty-one ports, and in every country we received a fantastic welcome. I would like to mention here an event that happened during this voyage.

§

The time was January 6, 1991. Our ship had departed from Port Kelang in Malaysia and was approaching the Strait of Malacca. It was a clear day. Abruptly Captain Wood's voice boomed out from the loudspeakers, "An American task force is coming towards us!"

I rushed up on the pontoon bridge with everybody. Since Iraq's invasion of Kuwait in August of 1990, world tension had been increasing day by day as nations drifted toward the Gulf War. Therefore, it is no surprise that the crisis posed a quandary for our maritime Silk Road project, a project that had as an important port of call Muscat, the capital of Oman in the Gulf. However, after the

---

[5] This Sindbad is the same as "Sinbad the sailor," the merchant in *the Arabian Nights* who made seven extensive voyages.
[6] Naniwa (modern Osaka) was the port from which Japan sent out missions to China during the Tang Dynasty, 618—907 A.D.

analysis of all kinds of information from the nations concerned (for example, the Gulf countries, America, and the Soviet Union) including the calculation of the range of Iraq's Scud missiles, it was my judgment, as well as Ambassador Musa's that Muscat was safe. We concluded that a large-scale war would not break out for several months. Because we were responsible for the lives of scores of scholars and journalists from many countries who would be aboard, our judgment in these circumstances was a very painful one. Finally, as originally planned, we had sailed from Venice on the 23rd of October 1990, accompanied by Federico Mayor, who was by now the Director General of UNESCO, and Mrs. Mayor. Venice celebrated our departure in an extraordinary variety of ways and even with an escort of beautifully festive gondolas of many colors.

On that day of January 6, in the Strait of Malacca under a blue sky, I witnessed a strange, even beautiful scene unfolding. At the distance of just 500 yards from our eastbound "Ark of Peace," we saw nineteen ships of the American Seventh Fleet in single-file formation coming west from the Philippines. We were going to meet and pass each other. Captain Wood, a British mercenary of the Sultanate, demonstrated the competence of the Royal Navy officer. When we met the American warships, he announced their names one by one as they passed on our left, gave us their numbers of officers and personnel, their navigational capacities and ranges, and the numbers of planes and helicopters they might carry. This amazed us all. When just the captain and I remained on deck, he calculated from the cruising speed of the American fleet the time of their arrival at the Strait of Hormuz in the Persian Gulf and informed me that it would be on January 15. I judged that the outbreak of war would be on January 16. (Actually, it came at dawn on January 17, 1991 and I watched it live on CNN.)

That encounter with the American fleet was a shocking occurrence. At that time, as UNESCO representative, I informed our science team leader that I wanted to give a special presentation at one of the seminars held twice a day on the ship. I told him the date of my communication would be January 16 and the theme would be "The Silk Roads and Peace."

Letter 2

The Silk Roads and Peace

(From a speech given on board Fulk Al Salamah, January 16, 1991)

Today I would like to speak to all of you on the soul of the Silk Road and to consider again what peace is. Concerning that route, we can see that strife on it did not cease. However, beyond the conflicts, there was dialogue between civilizations. This dialogue transcended the strife that occurred. Silk roads are points and lines, not a surface. Some people appear on those lines, and those people are thought to have contributed to the development of human civilization. There were things shared by these people, and that sharing can be said to constitute the soul of the Silk Road, as I see it. For me, trade on the Silk Road contains the following three features:

- *Travellers went searching, not selling (their object was precious goods, even ideas).*
- *They knew sharing, not monopoly.*
- *Trade was an international accomplishment achieved by people from many nations; it was not done by one nation alone.*

I think that these three points made possible not one-way traffic but two-way trade on the roads. In order to understand the relationship of these features of the Silk Road with the kind of peace which manifested itself as "Pax," I would like to set the stage for such understanding by reviewing once more, for all of us, the history of the Silk Road. Everyone needs to know it.

1. *Prehistory of the Silk Road*

The origin of the Silk Road hides behind the veil of time. Sea trade goes back at least 2,000 years before Christ. Meluha (now Pakistan), Magan (now approximately Oman), and Mesopotamia were connected by sea routes. In the tomb of the Egyptian Queen Hatshepsut (around 1500 B.C.) is recorded her order for fragrance from the southern extremity of the Arabian Peninsula in the region of Dhofar. A ship sailed down the Erythrae Sea (Red Sea) to get the perfume. Furthermore, in the remote ages of antiquity, it is thought that there was a north-south overland route. The indications are that there was a road stretching north from Egypt to Afghanistan. It might be called the "Road of Lapis Lazuli" or the "Jade Road." Lubo-Lesnichenko of the Hermitage Museum and Vadime Elisseeff of Paris produced evidence of this road. And the Scythians' splendid gold culture is thought to have merged with local gold when Hellenistic culture advanced northward across the Black Sea. However, whether to call these roads silk roads is another question. I think it more natural to consider silk routes as roads connecting East and West.

When we look at a map of Eurasia, the hard-to-cross mountain ranges run in the East-West direction. These are considered as pleats in the earth raised by the continental drift of the Indian plateau toward the north. For that reason, whether it's the Pamirs or the Tien Shan Mountain Range, one cannot pass through in a North-South way, but these pleated areas offer a topography in which people can go East or West. In the fifth century B.C. Herodotus describes Greek furriers who went to the Tien Shan area; they are thought to have gone along the steppe route from the Black Sea. As for the oldest production of silk goods, if we exclude the Russian theory which regards silk wares as already in the Ferghana[7] mounds of the 18th century B.C., we can, by a more conservative assessment of the evidence found in Altai, conclude that from at least the fifth to the third century B.C. silk was being made and transported westward on a road from China.

In brief, we should speak of the trade network connecting East and West throughout Eurasia as the Silk Road. At the same time it also becomes a road on which cultures can converse with each other, and this interaction is going to create human civilization in the historical sense.

---

[7] *Ferghana*, sometimes spelled *Fergana*, is described in *Micropaedia* in terms of the "Fergana Valley," which is mostly in eastern Uzbekistan and partly in Tajikstan and Kyrgyzstan, and is an "enormous depression between the Tien Shan and Gissar and Alay mountain systems." In the context of the present discussion, Ferghana should be thought of as a region. An important point in the area of Ferghana was Samarkand.

2. *The Silk Road*

If we focus on the statement by Ferdinand von Richthofen (1833—1905) about the *Seidenstrassen* (Silk Roads), namely, that the land route connected China and Persia, we can correctly say that it was opened in the 2nd Century B.C. by the Chinese Emperor Wudi of the Han Dynasty who sent his envoy by the route which lay north of the Tien Shan range. This emperor Wudi is the man who authorized Confucianism and established a monarchy. He sent his own man, Zhang Qian, to the country of Pegasus, the Heavenly Horse, to get an alliance with the Kushans[8]. The alliance was to help achieve a pincer attack upon the powerful Huns. Zhang Qian's first trip failed because the Huns captured him, but on the second try, he succeeded and returned home with "Heavenly Horses." This probably can be spoken of as recording the first Silk Road trip north of Tien Shan to Sogdiana (Samarkand in present-day Uzbekistan). But when we look West toward the Persian dynasty of Achaemenes (550—330 B.C.), Darius I had already conquered Egypt in the South and Sogdiana in the North, and even up to the river Indus in the East, thus opening up the way for the famous expedition of Alexander in the fourth century. Speaking of Alexander's expedition, not so well known is the fact that he took more than one hundred scholars with his army. We might guess that Alexander was searching for information about Indian thought and knowledge at that time. It seems to me the word Indus is derived from the Indo-Iranian word Sindhu meaning the great river. The people of that area came to be called Hindu (in Persian, Hendhu). In the Greek language, Indus is "Indos," and by that word the Indus Valley is also known. In terms of today's political geography, the "India" of that time would refer to the region of present-day Pakistan and the Indus River. Even Alexander's expedition had not crossed the main stream of the Indus River.

When we consider Persia or the area around the Indus River, the oceanic Silk Route is seen to be unexpectedly close. The "Navigation Chronicle of the Erythrae Sea" written in 60 A.D. at Alexandria states, "A road has been opened from the Ganges River to Bactria" (now

---

[8] It may help the reader to visualize the line up of empires from west to east. Draw the line from the Roman Empire in the West on through the Arsacid Empire (including Babylon) and the Kushan Empire in north India to the Han Empire of China.

Uzbekistan), thus linking the sea route and river route, and China appears by the name Cina. In the "Han History" it is written that in 166 A.D. a certain Emperor Andun of Rome had sent envoys to Hainan Island. Recently we have realized that this name refers to the Roman emperor Marcus Aurelius _Anton_inus[9] (second century A.D.). As for Emperor Wudi, by at least 111 B.C., he had dispatched a fleet from Canton to Southeast Asia and India.

3. *The Silk Road's "Bullet Train"*[10]

Time advances through the Tang, Sung, and Yüan periods. Chinese overseas trade reaches a peak, but this trade involves not only Chinese ships but also ships of India, Arabia, and so forth. In Arabia from the 8th century A.D., mainly in the shipbuilding yard of Sur in Oman, the workmen made the excellent dhow that came to play a leading role in the trade on the Indian Ocean. This is about the time that the Japanese Imperial Court, which had made Nara the capital, sent envoys nineteen times to Ch'ang-an (now Xian) in Tang China.

Now, at the beginning of the Ming Dynasty there were the great expeditions of Zheng He. Departing from Canton, these passed the Malacca Strait seven times from 1405 to 1424 going toward the Indian Ocean. His fleets were made up of several hundred ships that carried tens of thousands of soldiers making their crossings. They attacked Ceylon (Sri Lanka), and the expeditions extended as far as the Red Sea and the whole area of the east coast of Africa up to Madagascar. Zheng He, who was a Moslem, sent a division from his navy to the Persian Gulf and even to Mecca. I think that these great voyages were not intended for trade but rather to demonstrate recovery of sovereignty by the Han people from the Mongols and to restore Han authority and prestige in the world. It is a mystery why these extensive voyages, with ships several times as large as the caravel type of ships which Columbus used, were suddenly discontinued. In addition, the Ming Dynasty closed all ports and destroyed all Chinese records of these voyages. Also mysterious is the fact that these great voyages which preceded by several decades those of Columbus, Vasco da Gama, and Magellan, receive not a single line in Western textbooks.

---

[9] The "d" in Andun is pronounced in Mandarin like the "t" in Antoninus.

[10] Many Westerners call the swiftest state-of-the art rail system in Japan the Bullet train. The word "Shinkansen" denotes the same modern system as well as the historic route that provided its backbone.

After the 9th century the sea routes had taken the place of the land routes as the major path of the Silk Road. One reason is the danger that had arisen on the continental roads due to inland strife, but even more important was the development of advanced shipbuilding techniques. Merchant ships became larger and larger. In the Sung Period (10th to 13th centuries) we can see large ships capable of carrying even elephants. Also, the techniques of navigation developed so much that ships became able to go directly across the Indian Ocean carrying large quantities of materials in a short period of time. In modern terms, from this time the sea route was going to be the "Super Express" of the Silk Road.

Of course, we must not forget that the sea route also became a stage for conflict. For example, Rome's purpose was not to conquer all of Egypt but just Alexandria. This city had been a base for sea trade since the time of the Persian court of Achaemenes. Ships that departed from the Malabar Coast in India traversed the Red Sea and unloaded in Egypt. For a short distance camels carried the goods to Alexandria where cargo was reloaded and shipped to Rome. (It should be noted here that already in the 6th century B.C., Darius I was setting to work on the "Suez Canal.") Profits from import-export duties made Alexandria very rich. Rome, after the conquest of Alexandria in Cleopatra's time, became even richer.

I think that Chinese silk goods that appeared in Rome in the first century B.C. passed along this route. From the fact that Antoninus had sent envoys, we understand that the Roman people had already realized that there was a vast civilization known as "Cina"[11] in the East. However, since ships that departed from Indian ports carried goods via Alexandria, China and India were confused with each other so that the name "Seres" (meaning the country of silk) was given to both of these far away silk countries. We must also notice that there was a powerful country called Parthia (in the vicinity of present-day Iran, Iraq, and Syria) which was traversed by the land silk route. Because Parthia had a monopoly on the profits of this route, Rome bypassed it by sea to Kushan (India).

4. *The Structure Producing the Road*

Let us now try to consider the relationship between strife and the Silk Road; from that we may be able to infer something concerning

---

[11] *Cina* is Latin; the Greek is Cinae.

peace. Realistically, peace is not the absence of war or even everyone getting along well. There is a Latin word used by European scholars– *PAX*. In Japan Yoshiro Mutaguchi and others are introducing it, but I think we had better consider peace as manifested in PAX to be a kind of *high atmospheric pressure.*

There existed from the 2nd century B.C. until the end of the 3rd century A.D. what is called "Pax Romana." During this time the great Roman Empire controlled the whole area of the Mediterranean Sea. However, at the same time in the East where, as mentioned above, Wudi led the Han, another great empire existed. That is to say, there were two systems of high pressure, one in the East and the other in the West. Each of these centers of pressure pushed out toward the other, and the age of the Silk Road appeared.

Roads through the regions called the "western zone" by the Chinese had already been opened. This whole area corresponds to the Tarim Basin[12], the present-day area of Xinjiang Uygur and the northern and southern routes of the Desert of Death, Taklimakan. The roads going to Persia passed through the Pamir Plateau. The so-called Tien Shan North Road which led to the steppe route was also in use. From the other direction, Buddhism began to go east from Gandhara (now the northern part of Pakistan) entering the Tarim Basin. At about this same time, the "Sea route" also is thought to have become the usual way of linking Rome to India and Southern China.

This kind of phenomenon arises when the high pressure of two large cultural spheres exists in the East and West. The power of mutual attraction is at work in such cases. But in the period of "Three Kingdoms and Six Dynasties" of China (3rd to 5th centuries) this pressure weakens. Because of confusion within China, low pressure occurred everywhere.

The next period of Silk Road prosperity is the "Pax Islamica" period. It may be seen in the 7th to the 9th centuries. In the East it is the period of the Great Tang during which Ch'ang-an (Xian) served as capital. And in the West there was Constantinople, the capital of the

---

[12] *Tarim Basin.* "From the Tarim River, 1250 miles long, which flows eastward along the north edge of Taklimakan (Takla Makan), then SE into the region of Lop Nor. The basin is an area of about 350,000 square miles enclosed by Tien Shan, the Pamirs, and Kunlun Mountains . . . " Edited from *Webster's New Geographical Dictionary* (Merriam-Webster, Inc., 1984), p. 1188.

Byzantine Empire, the Umayya Dynasty in Syrian Damascus from 661 to 750, and in Baghdad the powerful Abbasside Dynasty (750—1258). Baghdad was the city that Caliph Al-Mansur built in 762.

This was the period when Islamic teaching spread explosively from the Middle and Near East on through North Africa to Iberia. The 8th to 9th centuries constituted the golden age of what is known in the West as the Saracen Empire. Linking this high-pressure system and that of the Tang in China during this time was the Silk Road. I would add that there was the Cordova Dynasty (756—1236), and the Granada Dynasty (1238—1492) on the Iberian Peninsula. Granada fell to the army of Queen Isabella of Castile in 1492. We should keep this year in mind, for this is the year when Columbus found a new continent.

During Pax Islamica the remarkable progress of shipbuilding techniques owed a lot to the Arabian people. Arab sailors performed some stunning feats. In the 8th century, Abu Udaida made a 5,000-mile voyage from Oman to Canton. This man is supposed to be the model for Sindbad the Sailor.

5. The Period "Pax Mongolica"

With the decline of this second period of two high-pressure systems, Silk Road trade also weakened. To see the arrival of the third period of the Silk Road we have to wait for the Yüan Dynasty (13th century). This is the period called "Pax Mongolica."

Urging his horse-riding troops ever forward as if he remembered the ancient Turkish migration route, the "Blue Wolf" Genghis Khan (1167—1227), conquered the whole area of Eurasia. His grandson, Kublai Khan (1215—1294), became the founder of the Yüan Dynasty in Peking. The Yüan period lasted from 1271 until 1368, as his clan formed successively other "Khan kingdoms." The Qipchâq Khan kingdom (1242—1502) extended from Moscow to the Eastern Europe of today. The kingdom of Il Khan (1258—1411) consisted of the territory of Persia, present-day Iran and Iraq.

Kublai also deployed his armies eastward to Korea, Annam (now Vietnam), Burma, and Java. How extensive his power and influence were can be understood from the following examples. Kublai's armies made two invasions into the harbor of Hakata in the northern part of Kyushu, Japan. The first was in 1274 and the second in 1281. On the first he sent 900 ships with 30,000 soldiers; on the second, 4,400 ships with 140,000 soldiers. The Kamikaze or Divine Wind sent this second force to the bottom of the bay. Although such a heavy defeat normally should halt everything, soon afterwards Kublai Khan successfully landed a large army on Java at Tuban (which we on this ship visited three days ago).   Incidentally, a royal family in this very same region defeated its rivals by using the Yüan (Mongol) troops cleverly.   The Majapahit Dynasty was born in this way.

Here I should urge you to notice that the high pressure of "Pax Mongolica" is qualitatively different from that of the Han and Tang periods.   The high pressure of the Han and Tang periods was matched by similar pressure in the West.   However, there was no balancing power anywhere to correspond to the Mongolian pressure.   The pressure from the Han and Tang had as its background their advanced cultures.   In the case of Mongols, however, their pressure consisted solely of the power of a great military nation so that the rulers had to learn from the ruled.   That is the difference.   Nevertheless, this Mongolian high pressure opened up transportation facilities.

In the 13th century Marco Polo used the overland route going and the sea route returning home.   Ibn Battuta of Morocco, by contrast, went by the sea route and returned by the land route.   Today how many visas would be necessary to make a trip of such a great distance?   At that time there was no such thing, but if Marco Polo had carried visas, how many would he have needed?   *Only one.*   That's because from Persia to Peking, all was Mongolian territory. The same was also true for the official envoys dispatched before Marco Polo, by the king of France and the Roman pope: John of Plano Carpini[13] (d. 1252) and William of Rubruck.   Marco Polo, a Venetian merchant and unofficial representative of Venice, returned to Il Khan, Persia, from Quanzhou (near Amoy) on the ship of Princess Cocachin, who was going to Il Khan to be married.   Though it was a very long journey, politically it was like a domestic trip.

In contrast to the Romans who are known as builders leaving their grand architecture everywhere, the Mongols are known as destroyers, and European countries very much feared attacks by the Tartars (Mongolian/Turkic tribes).   However, it would be unfair not to mention the Mongols' contribution to world civilization.   This horse-riding people, who used caravan sarai (relay stations) and horse relays,

---

[13] John of Plano Carpini, whom Britannica's *Micropaedia* identifies under his Italian name, "Giovanni da Pian del Carpini," was a Franciscan friar and first important European traveler in the Mongol Empire.   Pope Innocent IV sent him. His is the earliest noteworthy Western book on Central Asia.

developed the postal system. In fact, it was the Mongols who originated high-speed communication.

However, notwithstanding these positive contributions, the true spirit of the earlier Silk Road was becoming compromised during the Yüan Dynasty under the Mongols. In other words, we find their acts going against the three characteristics of the Silk Road which I mentioned at the beginning. One country unilaterally conquered and ruled. In one sense, Genghis and Kublai Khan showed the great European powers a model for their imperialism, which begins at the end of the 15th century.

6. What is Byzantium?

Since I have said that Genghis Khan proceeded west on the old Turkish road, I'm going to touch briefly on the Ottoman (Osman) Empire. It is thought that the Turkish people originally were born in the Altaic region near northern Mongolia. In Chinese, the same northern Turkish people are called by the name Turks. The Turkish people were to move gradually westward. After being settled for a long time along the Caspian shore, in the 13th century they moved to the Middle East. In 1258 they captured Baghdad. Then in 1453 they captured Constantinople, the last stronghold of Byzantium. They renamed it Istanbul and made it the capital of the Ottoman Empire. All neighboring countries including Greece were annexed to this empire. In the 15th – 16th centuries that influence was very powerful, and the siege of Vienna in 1525 is famous. I have heard that the bread called croissant was made in the shape of the half-moon flag (from the Islamic crescent) of the troops surrounding Vienna at that time. However, that siege would fail, and after the defeat by the Spanish navy at the sea battle of Lepanto in 1571, the Turkish Empire tended to decline.

The Topkapi Palace in the center of Istanbul was the palace of the Ottoman Empire. It enables us to dream about the splendid prosperity of these people. There we find 12,000 pieces of Chinese ceramics, mainly what the specialists call "Blue and White." We can suppose that these pieces were carried by the sea route to the Turkish-Byzantine realm. The Sultan sent the order for them to China. Huge jars of Japanese Imari porcelain are also on display. The thing I want to give attention to here is that the Ottoman Turks became a really great power after capturing the Byzantine area. Therefore, we must consider what Byzantium was that made it the object of Turkish conquest.

In 330 A.D. the Roman Emperor Constantine I moved the capital to Byzantium which in the future would be named Constantinople. In 395 Constantinople split from the Roman Empire and became the capital of the Eastern Roman Empire. It reached the peak of its prosperity in the 6th century. In the 8th century, it broke off relations with the Western Roman Empire because of the dispute over icons and iconoclasm. In the 9th—10th centuries, it prospered as the center of Greek Orthodoxy. In the 11th century the Seljuk Turks plundered the eastern part of the Eastern Roman Empire, but the Fourth Crusade in 1202—1204 recaptured Constantinople for a while. However, in 1453 it was finally occupied by Ottoman Turks and became an Islamic capital. In the history of civilizations, Byzantium occupied an important position. From the 4th to the 15th century, that is, for a span of ten centuries it was a great cultural center.

We must consider why Constantine I wanted to move the capital of the Roman Empire to Byzantium. "Light from the East" had been spoken of from ancient times, and about the time of the removal of the Roman capital, there were great cultural spheres to the east of Rome: Greece, Persia, India, and China. On the other hand, at that time there was almost nothing west of Rome. Therefore, the transfer of the capital, I think, meant a move toward a crossroads of civilizations. And, in fact, the encounter of cultures that met there on East-West and North-South axes contributed to the creation of the distinctive culture which we know as Byzantine.

7. The Beginning of "The Period of Western Europe"

The year 1500 marks a turning point of world history. The West had gained power and was replacing the East in dominance. It is correct to speak of the time from the 16th to the 20th century as "The Western Era." One part of that era is American independence.

The Silk Road changed greatly. No, we should rather say that it became something we cannot properly call the Silk Road. Portugal, Spain, Holland, and England came successively to send expeditions to Asia. The phenomenon occurred first as Pax Hispanica and then as Pax Britannica. Of England it was said, "The sun never sets on the British Empire."

The spirit of the age was to "enrich and empower your own country," so we would not wish to criticize one particular country. However, the way of trade that the great Western powers practiced at this time fundamentally differed from the spirit that had prevailed in the golden age of the Silk Road, though they travelled the same sea routes.

First, I must mention "the lack of a spirit of dialogue." That deficiency involved both the conquest by power and the subordination of spirit. As I mentioned in the beginning, the Silk Road was originally a road on which "everyone went seeking something good." Even if colonies were exporting to the home country, we cannot say that there was equal flow both ways. It was only a one-way flow. When we speak about two-way flow, it implies that each party respects the other nation and culture. A Persian caravan party was seeking silk while a Chinese ship was seeking perfume or spice. By imperial command in Ch'ang-an (modern Xian) a Moslem mosque was built to welcome the merchants from Persia. Also Xuen Zhang, a Chinese travelling monk of the 7th century, brought back from India original Buddhist sutras (holy texts) that were translated at the Great Wild Goose Pagoda associated with the Temple of Benevolent Grace in Xian.

We have earlier said that in the 13th century Genghis Khan showed an example of conquest by military might, but even this Mongol learned from other cultures—and other religions. In contrast, Western nations put their own "god" first. An example of this attitude is the slogan of those who became the conquistadors of South America with their three G's of God, Glory, and Gold. God became like an imperial banner for the army, and the army became the guard for traders.

Of course, Asian nations had their own long histories and distinctive cultures, and, most importantly since they had large populations, none became extinct as did the Inca Empire. However, the colonization of Asia and that of South America cannot be said to be essentially different. Here I see a spiritual stigma bequeathed by the Crusades. "The sword and the Koran," is the phrase by which Christians have judgmentally summarized Islam, but wherein do the methods of Christians in the colonial centuries differ? If they differ at all, isn't it because the earlier intense faith of Christians had faded?

Secondly, it is said that there was "a lack of the spirit of sharing" in this period. Trade on the Silk Road was a "sharing" trade. Every harbor city and every caravan city stood to profit because goods were transshipped from each. In short, sailors and their ships from Arabia, India, China, and so forth, constituted a relay system. That is how an imaginary country like "Seres" was born. It was a kind of symbiosis or way of "living together." The history of the caravan-*sarai* (caravan inns) also tells of "living together." The lord of every city built a *sarai*. The traders and other travellers could stay there free of charge for three days. That is because the lord knew that the passing of the caravans was a profitable, even a divine blessing. We must not overlook the fact that these caravan-*sarai* were great information centers.

Marco Polo and Ibn Battuta are exceptional persons who made the whole long itinerary using these caravan inns. Were their journeys successful from the point of view of commerce? No, they left only chronicles. We must note that neither Venice nor Morocco sent out missions to follow up. The cities that sent these representatives out to China knew that in the long run a system of relay stations that involves cooperating with other nations and cities was commercial wisdom. It would prove to be counterproductive for one country to make a profit of ten or twenty times on an investment.

The East India companies, which were set up in some European countries from the 17th century on, acted against this wisdom from ancient times. Their principle was monopoly. They tried to monopolize the trade on all routes for themselves; that is, they tried to keep the twenty-fold advantage to themselves. To protect these profit-making routes, the great powers of the West opened the way to the world wars of the future by their exchange of naval battles, their seizing of rival countries' ships, and so on.

In the third place, the Great Powers wiped out "trade depending on multicultural, multinational teams." Their own nation's ships, army, and merchants took the place of the ships and caravans in which various nations shared rides with each other. This phenomenon appears just at the time the so-called "modern state" was established in many Western Nations. In other words, during modern times "national" replaced "international." The modern state cannot be separated historically from the extension of colonialism.

8. *The Three Waves of Colonialism*

This colonialism had three waves. The first wave belonged to the period of ascendancy of Portugal, Spain, and Holland. Next came the wave of England and France. America, which robbed Spain of the Philippines, also joined this wave. And later, in the third wave, came Germany, Italy and Japan who were late in starting their own colonial experiments.

Therefore, I think the Second World War II was essentially a war of the third wave colliding with the second at the same time that the second wave hit the first. The problem is not that of military winners and losers but that all three waves had a spiritual constitution that was fundamentally opposed to that of the Silk Roads. No matter how just the causes that were advocated (for example, the Great East Asian Co-Prosperity Sphere, or the protection of democracy), the issue finally boils down to colonialism's struggle over the same lands. After World War II, two high-pressure zones emerged that were poles apart and could be called the "Pax Russo-Americana." But since they constituted a balance of terror, no road ran between them. And with the collapse of the Berlin Wall, we have entered the era of "Pax Americana." A single high pressure has occurred before, but we must pay careful attention to this phenomenon. If we look at things historically, a period of two high-pressure centers could continue at peace for a relatively long time. Contrary to that, the peace of Pax Mongolica collapsed in only one century. Doesn't this suggest that a single high-pressure system depending on military power is easily broken? In contrast, the Byzantine Empire, which existed as a cultural core more than a military power, prospered across more than ten centuries.

Riding together on the Ark of Peace, like Silk Road travellers of ancient times, we have become forgetful that we represent more than 30 nationalities. At all ports of call we have not only taught but also learned many things. Today when a hot war may begin at any time, I have wanted, as far as my understanding allowed, to communicate to all of you "The Soul of the Silk Road."

§

My friend, as I spoke the above words, the ship was rolling so much that in order to stand up I had to catch hold of the edge of a table. However, my tense thoughts and feelings at that time made me forget being seasick, and I was able to speak from my heart. I was vaguely beginning to see that "the heart of the Silk Road" is becoming the prototype of our own future road.

It must be a road based on neither the "logic of war" nor the "culture of war" as were the three waves of colonialism. The future road must not succumb to the old colonial imperative "to propagandize, to rob, and to rule," but it should manifest, rather, a mentality disposed toward a "culture of peace" that will prevail in the future. Such a culture will be led by the desire "to learn, to give, and to share." Only this spirit will make possible the coexistence of humankind upon this limited planet. Those were the thoughts passing through my heart on that fateful day.

Letter 3

Sindbad's Country, Oman

Dear Friend,

It is said that Queen Hatshepsut of Egypt sent her fleet to the Red Sea around 1500 B.C., having ordered fragrance from the land of Dhofar at the Southern extremity of the Arabian Peninsula. That was also the same fragrance the Queen of Sheba offered King Solomon (almost 500 years later). It is called frankincense and can be obtained from a shrub grown in the highlands back of the ancient city of Salalah that is near the border between Oman and Yemen. (In this same area today, ruins have been discovered by satellite that are regarded as being those of Ubar or Iram of the 2nd century B.C., which are mentioned in the Koran.)

In the making of frankincense, a tree is scratched, as in gathering from gum trees. The sap falls and hardens like pine resin. When we put it in a clay pot and light it, it will blaze up. At first, black smoke comes out and it does not smell very good. However, the moment after the flame is extinguished, the smoke changes to white and a sweet scent comes into the air. When I smelled the fragrance, right away I realized that it was not my first experience. Of course, it is the incense used in the Mass of the Roman Catholic Church.

Along with copper, which had also been produced in this land, this perfume was used in Mesopotamia as something of great value. It was carried to many countries of the Near and Middle East and then to Rome. At the time of Jesus' birth, it is said that one of the articles of tribute brought by the three magi from the East was this frankincense. My friend, if that is true, it would be no wonder if this fragrance was wafted through the churches in Gaul (ancient name for France).

Oman, located at the exit point of the Persian Gulf, is a country destined to live always facing the sea. The country is covered by rocky mountains and deserts; moreover, there is no river that can be considered a real river. There are only forests of date trees. However, in this barren land, we suddenly see clear water running in a rock-formed canal. This is called *falaj*. It is made according to the irrigation technology brought from Persia during the period from the third to the seventh century. When a spring of water is discovered on the side of a mountain, not even one drop of it is wasted. It is guided for surprising distances, in certain places by waterways paved with stone on the surface of the earth and in other places by underground conduits that go even under dry riverbeds (wadis). The Persians disseminated this wonderful irrigation technology, which in ancient Persia was called "*qanat*" or "*kâriz,*" to many places on the Silk Road. It is found as far away as the northern and southern Tien Shan routes in the Tarim Basin in China.

By means of ocean trade, Oman formed a great empire from the 7th to the 15th century. I want to mention Abu Udaida who actually sailed 4,400 miles (7,000 kilometers) in the 8th century, crossing the India Ocean, passing through the Malacca Strait, then north on the South China Sea to Canton (Guangzhou). Canton has the oldest mosque in China. Oman sailors got used to linking the Persian Gulf with India, Southeast Asia, and China in the East, as well as with various places on the east coast of Africa.

Zanzibar, which is now united with Tanzania to form the United Republic of Tanzania, was a great base in the South for Oman. On this east African coastal island of Zanzibar where we can enjoy Arabian fragrances, even now the sheiks are the descendants of the sultans of Oman. In this united country, the sheik of Zanzibar has the distinction of serving as first prime minister.

As early as the 8th century A.D. the ports of the Maritime Silk Route in the Arabian Sea were Sohar (Muscat), Qalhat, and Hormuz. Chinaware of the Song period has been unearthed at these sites.

§

Why did the sea routes take the place of the overland silk roads after the 9th century? The many wars in central Asia and the uneasiness about public security in inland China were surely factors. However, I think that this change would not have occurred without the invention in Arabia at this time, especially by the shipbuilders of Oman, of the V-shaped keel, exactly the keel used by modern yachts that presently compete for the America's Cup. The ship they had invented was at the forefront of shipbuilding technology in those days. By its use of the monsoon or seasonal wind called "the wind of Hippalos" (already known in the first century A.D.), the triangular-masted dhow did not need to use a coastal route. It could cross oceans directly. Of course, astronomy, in which the Arabians had specialized, supported these direct crossings. To progress to the East, they are supposed to have oriented themselves with the Polar Star 90 degrees to their left. In this manner, the sea route, as shaped by Arabian dhows, became the "Shinkansen" (Bullet Train) of the Silk Road. In contrast, around this same time, one third of the ships carrying Japanese missions to the Tang Dynasty vanished in the rough waves of the East China Sea because they had flat bottoms like river boats. The children of Oman are taught that the Sindbad who turns up in *The Arabian Nights* is from Sohar in their country. It is even said that the already-mentioned Abu Udaida was the model for this character, but, as may be expected, it is not clear whether this is someone who had a real existence or one who appears only in collections of sailor legends. However, it is certain that these tales are based on information from the real history of navigation.

At the end of the 1970's, when the young English explorer Tim Severin set up a program to reproduce a 9th-century Arabian ship to sail to China, Oman's Minister of Cultural Heritage willingly assisted in the project. Tim Severin is the person who some years before, after reading an ancient document "Navigatio" found in the London Library, became convinced that the 6th-century Irish monk Brendan reached North America by crossing the North Atlantic in a leather-covered boat; Severin faithfully repeated that voyage. He also reproduced the return sea trip of Alexander the Great's army from the Indus River and most recently proved the probability of a Pacific crossing by the Chinese envoy Xufu of the Qin (Chin) Dynasty in the third century B.C. In Oman's city of Sur, which still builds the dhow by traditional methods, Tim Severin's boat was fashioned from Indian lumber and coconut-fiber rope and was named "Sohar." In 1980, Severin, with sailors from Oman, crossed the Indian Ocean, fighting sharks on the way. Having overcome the rough South China Sea, he arrived in Hong Kong. Thus he had resurrected in a wonderful way the journey of Sindbad the sailor.

1980 also marked the 10-year commemoration of the accession to the throne of the sovereign of Oman, Sultan Qaboos bin Said al-Said. At the 20-year commemoration, UNESCO's project "Integral Study of the Silk Roads," used the ship named Fulk al Salamah owned by this same Sultan Qaboos.

§

When you go to Oman what strikes you is the coexistence of the medieval with the 20th-century version of "modern." The contrast is almost too great between the highways in today's capital area and the Nizwa castle (included in UNESCO'S World Heritage list) or the remains of the citadel of Bahla surrounded by a kind of "great wall."

Prince Qaboos, after he returned from study abroad in England and was confined by his father in a castle in Salalah, resolved to modernize his country. Up to that point, the country had been frozen in time for a long period. But where do you think Sultan Qaboos receives VIPs of foreign countries? In a tent in the desert. For the desert is the protector of the holy traditions of the Arabs and is thought to preserve the purity of their language and blood.

§

My friend, there are many ironies in history. The greatest irony, however, probably occurred in 1498 when the sailor Ahmed bin Majid of Oman, with his sea charts and compass, taught Vasco da Gama the sea route around the southern tip of Africa and guided the Portuguese sailor to Ahmed's own sea, the Indian Ocean. This permitted Westerners to discover what is called the Indian route. Nine years later the Portuguese fleet occupied Muscat, next Goa on the opposite side of the ocean, and then the kingdom of Malacca, in this way raising the curtain on the colonial period. Ahmed could not have known that his act of goodwill would become a revolutionary pivot of history.

Also, the Jesuits, who appointed Francis Xavier as their first missionary, followed in the footsteps of the Portuguese. Stirred by the tales of Marco Polo, they aimed their efforts toward the great countries of Cathay and Zipangu (Japan). After 1500 A.D. the West succeeded to the place of premier importance which the East had previously held. That African cape is even now ironically called the Cape of Good Hope.

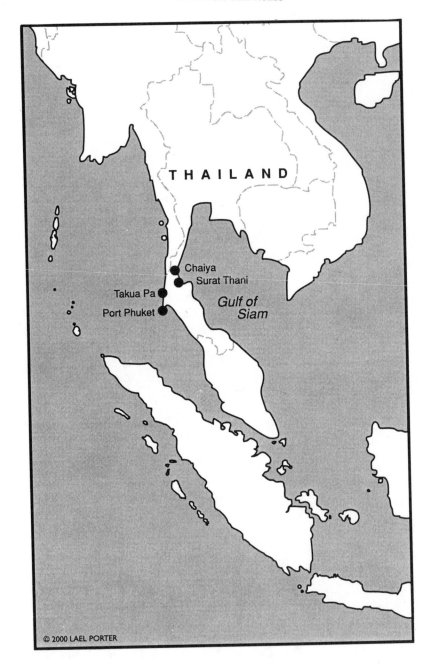

© 2000 LAEL PORTER

Letter 4

The Phantom Kingdom of Srivijaya

Dear Friend,

I had heard from the late Professor Tsuguo Mikami that there seems to have been an East-West route which crossed through the center of the southern part of the Malay Peninsula (Isthmus of Kra) in Thailand. It was the route that connected Chaiya, situated on the Gulf of Siam on the east of Thailand, with Takua Pa that faced the Andaman Sea on the west of Thailand.

Since what he said was unforgettable, in undertaking to draft the "Integral Study of Silk Roads: the Sea Route" I included his two spots (Takua Pa and Chaiya) on the route of our ship. While preparations were under way, the Thai committee reported that on the Takua Pa side we could use Port Phuket, which is approximately 45 miles south, but there was no harbor at all for the 11,000-ton "Fulk al Salamah" on the Chaiya side. So we had to give up this site.

However, in November of 1990, on the occasion of the international seminar in Muscat, Oman, when I spoke of this concern to the Thai archeologist Kemchat, he suddenly leaned forward and said, "I am also investigating that matter, myself. Many interesting things are being unearthed in the mountains around there." We chatted for hours about his essay's manuscript including the illustrative plates. And before leaving, he said, "When I go home I'll consult with my board in Thailand to find out if a journey is possible for the royal yacht team."

On Christmas day of 1990, I was on the ship sailing from Madras. As the ship was passing safely through the Bay of Bengal in its approach to the Andaman Sea, something happened which I didn't think possible. In a fax printout, imagine our surprise to see inserted in the updated schedule at Phuket the words: "Takua Pa to Chaiya Route"! Moreover, with a night at Surat Thani, we could spend two days doing that. This "sea route passing through land" is actually a land route originally connecting sea portions of the Silk Road for the ancient merchants.

Although Phuket is known only as a popular tourist destination, at one bound it gained status as a base for a UNESCO science group to investigate the "phantom route." Together with Professor Noburu Karashima of the University of Tokyo, who was on board with us as a representative of Japanese specialists, I shared the joy of being able to traverse this unknown route.

§

On December 29 of 1990, a "Special Exhibition on the Maritime Silk Road" was held for us in the National Museum at Phuket. The cramped quarters were jam packed with articles excavated from the coast of the Andaman Sea: gods and goddesses of Hinduism, Buddha images, Chinese pottery, bars of a gold-copper alloy, bead jewelry from India, bells from Quanzhou on the coast of southern China, huge Donson drums from northern Vietnam, and so forth. I looked at these wondrous things while worrying about diarrhea. A large stone statue of Vishnu caught my eye. It is said that this was unearthed from the mountain near Takua Pa, and even today in this area the images of Ganesha and different Devas[14] are buried in holes at the base of growing trees.

The next day we are at last leaving for Chaiya. First of all, the scenery on the route across the peninsula deserves our attention. There was a rugged range of mountains that made one think of Guilin (Kweilin) in China, and within them are countless caves. A person hunting for swallow nests discovered the colored wall paintings that have been in the caverns near Phangnga and Krabi on the east coast of Thailand since ancient times. Amazingly, there is even a picture of a Dutch (or Portuguese?) ship. It seems that until quite recently there were people living in these caves.

In the Surat Thani district where the town of Chaiya is located, the Srivijaya style Mahayana temples of Wat Long and Wat Kaeo show the connection with Sumatra and Java. At the Chaiya Museum we again saw many items from many lands just like those at Phuket. The existence of the sea route of cultural exchange is unquestionable because the same types and age of artifacts were found on both sides of

---

[14] *Deva.* In Hindu mythology a god or spirit.

the Malay Peninsula. I realized that through this neck of land called the Isthmus of Kra, Arabia and India were historically connected to China.

§

We had our greatest feeling of deep emotion, however, on the deserted Laem Pho seashore of Chaiya. There I caught sight of a shard. Mr. Karashima cried out, "Changsha of the Tang Dynasty!" (Changsha was one of the most popular types of ceramics during the Tang period. Pieces of it were made to order for the imperial court.) "Look here!" I called as I picked up three shards. When I turned around, I saw Mr. Karashima quickly splash into the shallows to search through the sand of the sea floor. I went back to our hut to deposit my shards. Surprise! Within less than thirty minutes, the team members were vying with each other to bring in other shards, and right before our eyes their findings were piling up like a mound in our temporary shed. They were all from the Tang period (618-907), when Ch'ang-an (modern Xian) was the capital. There were no exceptions. Representatives of the Thai Department of Archeology who were accompanying us kept these shards, but I was allowed to take as a memento the first piece I found.

This was a decisive experience in my life. There was excited discussion with the Thai specialists Amara, Srishichat, Pitiphat, and others, as well as with Professor Prematillake of Sri Lanka, and the American bead-specialist Mr. Francis. Joining them for the discussion were Noboru Karashima and Sigeru Ikuta. These exchanges altered somewhat our view of silk route history.

§

Tang ships possibly reached the vicinity of Surat Thani in the 7th century. A Chinatown may even have been built near the mouth of the Mekong River at that time. Indians had come sailing in Arabian dhows and settled in the area of Takua Pa. From a central mountain range, two streams flow. One goes down the west side towards Takua Pa and another flows eastward to Surat Thani. Indians used "the rivers" for exchanges between Takua Pa and Surat Thani. When the rivers were used, the route going over the mountain pass was about 30 miles long. An early hypothesis that elephants were used to pull the traders' boats across the mountains is not realistic. A relay system made good sense because a trader could in this way entrust his load to sailors navigating familiar seas on both sides of the Malay Peninsula. To take a whole ship over the pass would only make the load heavier and destroy all hope of profit. So, the most reasonable hypothesis now is that boats from India unloaded their shipments at Takua Pa. These goods were carried by riverboats up to the mountains and transferred to elephants to cross the pass. Finally they were loaded on to riverboats on the other side to go down stream. Eventually boats bound for China took on the loads for the last leg of the relay.

I think that Islam also passed along this route. In the village Phumriang near Surat Thani on the east coast, an ancient silk industry still thrives, and the residents are all followers of Islam.

Now returning to the other side, we find Takua Pa facing the Andaman Sea. Takua Pa is at present a small fishing village, but its bay would allow use as a harbor. It could accommodate ocean-going ships and would therefore attract sailors. The island now called Ko Ko Kao was in ancient times a foreign colony. Mr. Karashima points out that the town built on the island was indeed the idea of foreign people. He and I decided to borrow a small boat to go to see the island. As soon as team members knew of the plan, at least fifteen of them came to crowd aboard. Because the water came higher than the waterline[15] on the boat, we could not safely land on the island that had no pier or much of anything else. Afterwards, however, the photographer Ms. Toby Molenar, having borrowed another boat to go to Ko Ko Kao, found there a porcelain shard for me. It was indeed Tang pottery and even of the same color as the one I had found on the other side of the peninsula.

§

Why was this mixed overland and river route used instead of simply going around Singapore? I suppose that it was probably to avoid the hotbed of pirates in the Strait of Malacca. (Incidentally, these pirates appear even today. There was the report of a pirate raid on a merchant ship just six months before our voyage. Therefore, as we passed through the strait, our captain had machine guns ready on both sides of the ship.) Or perhaps as Captain Wood mentioned, since the monsoons blew in the same way on both sides of the peninsula, it would be

---

[15] *Waterline* is a nautical term referring to the line drawn on the side of a ship or boat to show where the water should come when the boat is safely loaded. If water is above such a line, the boat is in danger of sinking.

difficult for a ship then driven only by tail winds to make that journey. The overland shortcut might be the faster route, as well as the safer.

A mystery, however, still remains. Why was this route discontinued a thousand years ago in the Sung period (just after the Tang Dynasty)? We know the trade did continue by other routes because Sung celadon porcelain has been excavated in Arabia, India, and Sri Lanka. In relation to this, at a seminar in Bangkok, Mr. Srishichat of Thailand announced that there were at least five crossing routes in the southern part of the peninsula, though the sites have not yet been investigated. In particular, he says the most valuable sites to research lie in the Kedah area at the northern end of Malaysia near Thailand.

For me the history of Srivijaya is connected with this. The capital of this mysterious kingdom is not just Palembang on Sumatra. To be exact, it was "a wandering kingdom." According to some explanations, it was sometimes centered at Jambi and occasionally at Kedah or Chaiya. During its most prosperous period, when this kingdom possessed the whole area from Sumatra to the Malay Peninsula, the Strait of Malacca became its inland sea. At that time, they could station the royal navy in this sea, collect pertinent duties in the harbor cities, and develop the best plans for controlling pirates. If they successfully accomplished these things, all of their trading ships could round Singapore and enter Palembang. Additionally, the transshipment by river to Surat Thani might not be profitable for ships which became too large after the 10th century. When the Malaka Kingdom came into being at the beginning of the 15th century, it is said that the prince of that emerging kingdom came from Palembang. Malaka covered much of the territory of old Srivijaya and continued to provide a safe sea route.

Letter 5

Memory of the People

Friend: Just as individuals have their own memories, isn't it true also that whole peoples can have their collective memories? I came to consider that possibility because of various experiences on the Silk Road of the Seas.

My first thoughts on this came when I visited the Gulf States. Since their oil boom of 1973 (an oil shock for the West) these countries quickly became prosperous. For example, Bahrain is a small country with more than half the population consisting of immigrants. There are the "Bahrainis," that is, the citizens of Bahrain; they became the "new nobility" who employ two or three servants (drivers, maids, and the like). In certain locations of the capital city, Al-Mānamah, rows of splendid buildings have sprung up in places where formerly there was nothing. Since the civil war in Beirut, every international bank has moved its headquarters for the Near and Middle East to Bahrain. Shiny automobiles are on the increase, and the place is overflowing with Japanese electrical appliances. We noticed many people whose faces have an Indian appearance. They are Pakistanis; the women are housemaids. Filipinos are serving in restaurants.

A change that suddenly occurred in this society beginning with the latter half of the 70's has caused a strange phenomenon. The rate of infant deaths has doubled. Although life generally has improved, why has such a thing happened? The explanation of the on-the-spot UN representatives goes like this: European food manufacturers brought in a large quantity of powdered milk and advertised that in the "civilized" countries there is a tradition of nursing infants on the bottle. The Bahraini women had originally been desert people, but since they became modern ladies, they stopped breast-feeding their babies and started using the "child-rearing methods of the West." Moreover, they let the Pakistani maids use these new methods. But because they did not have the modern concept of sanitation, they did not disinfect either the bottles or the water used to feed the babies. UN officials said that TV ads advertising the powdered milk in this situation were a form of murder.

This matter reminds me of the large number of infant deaths that occurred in the Cambodian refugee camps. The powdered milk was supposed to be emergency help, but unless it was accompanied by drinkable water and sanitary utensils as well as people who could teach sanitation, it could end up becoming as lethal an instrument as poison gas. And it did.[16]

§

Let us return to the topic I was discussing. What I was considering in the Persian Gulf had to do with the mother countries of the immigrant laborers. If we study recent history, we can understand why Algerians came to France or why Turks went to Germany. But when the oil dollars accumulated in Arabia, why would people from the Near and Middle East NOT come while from farther away large numbers of Pakistanis and Filipinos, DID come? We understand why Hindu Indians would not come to Bahrain while Islamic Pakistanis would come, but the Filipino immigrants do not include many, if any, Muslim believers from the southern island of Mindanao which is populated by many Muslims. The Filipinos are from Manila and are probably Catholic Christians. Besides, many South Koreans are coming as technicians. These also have no relationship to Islam.

I noticed one thing in Oman. The mother countries of these immigrants are ALL ones we put on the itinerary of the Fulk al Salamah, in other words, "on the maritime Silk Road." Also, the countries from which people come to Japan —Korea, China, Thailand, the Philippines, India, and Pakistan—are all countries visited by our sea route study ship.

---

[16] We cannot qualify every social criticism put forward in this book, but, in the interests of both clarity and fairness regarding the comparison with poison gas, we must add one qualification here: ". . . except that poison gas is administered with the intent to kill while powdered milk is distributed with a mixture of goodwill, greed, oversight, ignorance, administrative incompetence, and haste."

Friend, the "Sea Road" was a genuine road. Because of the existence of this road, the people who live on this line move when wealth accumulates somewhere on the road. Migration is not so much a problem of geographical distance as of the existence of a route. Of course, the individual immigrant laborers probably do not have this kind of awareness of available routes. It is customary for some families to send one of their members to work away from home. What I see in effect here, however, is the "memory of people" whose ancestors have followed the road over a period of ten centuries. "People's memory"— when I got this concept I realized that it was going to solve many of the questions and puzzles in my mind.

This matter is not limited to the Sea Road. There is something that seems to be clearly sculpted into the "monkey stones," which may be seen in the village of Asuka, south of Nara, the ancient capital of Japan. Among these sculptures are some statues clearly showing "Foreign Figures," *kojin*. During the Tang Dynasty in China this word referred to "people from the West" (Persians), as it did in Japan. Many Persians were living in Xian, China, and I understand from this sculpture in Nara that at least in the 7th century A.D., Persians came to the area of Nara, probably by way of China. There are also *kojin* masks to be found in the imperial storehouse of Shōsōin[17], also in Nara. Furthermore, in the same storehouse there are Persian glass products that date back to the 5th century. I feel that when we become aware of the silk routes we have a basis for understanding why so many of the immigrants coming into present-day Japan are from Persia (today's Iran) while people from Iran's neighbors such as Syria and Afghanistan haven't come to Japan.

For example, in regard to the Mongolian army as it swept across Eurasia in the 13th century, the question is, "With what kind of objectives and on what kind of roads did these people pass?" The Mongolians have a kinship with the Turkish folk (Türk) whose home is

---

[17] The *Shōsōin,* a wooden storehouse, was built in Nara in 756. It has escaped fire for more than 1200 years. It was opened only by explicit order of the emperor. Even the most powerful shoguns could not bypass this requirement. As a result, as Papinot says, "it has reached the present day unimpaired, and is actually an archaeological museum of inestimable value." E. Papinot, *Historical and Geographical Dictionary of Japan* (Tokyo: Tuttle, 1972; reprinted from its first edition in 1910), p. 591.

the Altai mountain range. These Turkish folk were moving on the steppe route farther and farther to the west, taking ten centuries or so in the process. Finally they reached Anatolia and then the territory of modern Turkey. When you look at this route on an ordinary world map, it seems that they made a great detour. But when you study a globe, this route is almost a straight line in a belt stretching from Xinjiang Uygur (in China) on through Kazakhstan, Uzbekistan, Turkmenistan to Byzantium (modern Turkey), thus forming what I call the "Turkish Road."

Furthermore, the Hun clans of the same Mongolian lineage also migrated westward and, having crossed the Ural Mountains, reached Hungary. Tulips, the flower of Central Asia, reached Holland through Turkey in the 17th century. These same Altaic people brought with them the Heavenly God concept when they arrived in Japan via Manchuria and the Korean peninsula. (I will deal with this matter in more detail in a future letter.)

It is not too well known that the Thai people are also descendents of the Mongolians. Since Mongolians had southbound roads to Tibet and other such places, I find that, after staying in Yunnan Province in China for a while, they entered today's peninsula of Indochina along the Mekong River. There they mingled and also fought with the natives such as the Khmer and Burmese. At last they settled in the place where they now are. The Thai dynasty was established at Sukhothai in the 13th century, and after that, moves gradually south to Ayutthaya and now Bangkok.

The southeastern silk road that stretched from Yunnan to Burma (Myanmar) has begun to receive attention quite recently, but Annam (now Vietnam) also has a relationship with Yunnan, and it is thought that the latter links up with the whole of Central Asia. The reasonable conclusion is that the people linked by lines across this vast region are not the settled ones such as the Han but the horse-riding people, the Mongolian-related people. Exactly comparable were the camel-riding Persians who became the key actors on the silk roads in the West. We must not forget the fact that Sumatra and Java, through Srivijaya, linked Malaysia, Thailand, Laos, Cambodia, and Vietnam into one unified body.

Genghis Khan and Kublai Khan, who attained their fame in the 13th century, were aiming at something somewhere, but what and where? To the West, it was the Turkish road, the route of the Turkish people. And to the East, it was the Altaic route from Manchuria to the Korean peninsula and across the Sea of Japan to Hakata. This Japanese city had earlier sent out envoys to Tang China and to Silla (an ancient kingdom of Korea). To the south, as stated, the Mongolians had their route to Annam, Java, and Burma. When we look at these destinations, we can understand the Mongolian invasion as being, after all, a reminiscence of their "people's memory."

§

Friend, when it was decided that the port of call of the Fulk al Salamah (our sea-route research ship) was not to be Palembang on Sumatra but Surabaya on the eastern tip of Java, my mind was already flying to Tuban which could be easily visited from Surabaya. It is the place where Kublai Khan's navy landed. At that same place, during the Second World War, the Japanese Navy landed. In between times, it had been a base for the Dutch East India Company.

In the 14th century, when Muslims captured Java, the Hindu faction of the Majapahit Dynasty escaped to the island of Bali. A clan of its last princess occupied the sacred volcano Bromo. If you spend all night climbing the sacred mountain on horseback, you can worship the sunrise at the top. In their desperate effort to survive, these refugees terraced their fields up to the tops of the surrounding hills.

Surabaya of Indonesia, along with Quanzhou in China, were the places that most enthusiastically welcomed our marine Silk Road research ship. I cannot forget the Indonesian scenes that are seared into my brain. Even before our ship could touch shore, there began musical performances by troupes of more than a thousand ethnically costumed dancers and musicians. Decorated elephants came out to the pier to welcome us. I see even now the exquisite *Mahabharata* dance performed at the evening reception.

And I compare all this with the scene at Quanzhou, in China, where masses of welcoming people clogged two kilometers of our road to the Islamic mosque. The city of Quanzhou—that is, Zaitun mentioned by Marco Polo and Ibn Battuta—amazed us by building a special pier where our research ship could touch shore. Their enthusiasm was such that they even erected a museum for the Silk Road of the Sea. It opened on the day our ship arrived. I noticed that here Manichaeism, Nestorianism, and Islam had been introduced from far-away Persia.

In the itinerary prepared by the Indonesian research team, there was provision for an international seminar such as we had at each of our 21 ports of call. There were scheduled visits to museums and to historic ruins near Surabaya, but a visit to Tuban was not included. Therefore, from our ship as it approached Surabaya, I sent this telegram: "Wish by all means you include historic harbor city of Tuban." After I arrived in Surabaya and conferred with national committee-chairman Dr. Soepoyo, this visit to Tuban was hurriedly inserted into the last day's schedule.

The city of Tuban only had 48 hours to prepare to receive our international study team. However, when we got there, we saw the city hall decorated with beautiful flowers. It was filled with music and young girls dancing in colorful native costumes representing all regions of the country. Everyone was doing their best to make up for the shortness of time. Even the harbor ships were fully decked out. And at the ends of the jetties we were astonished to see colorful Mongol soldiers flying high their symbol of the 13th-century Mongol dynasty imprinted on triangular flags! And I mustn't forget the grand welcoming ceremony at the Chinese temple.

Friend, when I come to Indonesia, I really feel "nostalgia" here. I can almost think of it as being my own far-away homeland. *Adat*, the unwritten common law of the people of Indonesia, is something infinitely close to our Japanese "mind of *wa*" (peace, harmony, unity). Indeed, the Indonesians use *Adat* to unify this country which has as many languages as there are days in a year. My thoughts, as I stood on the seashore of Tuban, ran far and fast to the "sea road": Man goes to places where the road runs. That road is engraved in the deep unconscious layer of the memory of the people.[18]

---

[18] The reader may see a similarity here to Jung's concept of a collective unconscious, but Jung did not talk about the "Routes."

Letter 6

The Sky is Black—the Northern Route

Friend,

In Central Asia we see many place-names to which the prefix *kara* or *khara* is attached. Among them is the 22,000-foot-high Karakoram Range which lies in front of a road that stretches from Pakistan's upper valley of Hunza to Khotan and Kashgar in northwest China. Far away in Outer Mongolia there is Karakoram city where Genghis Khan had his base camp. Then also: Kharakhoto (black city) in the western part of Inner Mongolia; Karakash, river of black jade, which flows north from the Kunlun mountain range to the Taklimakan Desert; the Karakum Desert of western Turkmenistan; and, finally, even the name of a dynasty, the Karakhan.

That this "*kara*" means "black" I have known before, but it was during my conversations with Professor Otkan whom I met on the route for the Integral Study of the Silk Roads that I learned the fact that this black "is not ordinary black." My conversation with this scholar of Asian studies from Ankara University ran as follows:

Otkan: Mr. Hattori, do you know why the Black Sea and the Red Sea are so named? In reality both are blue.

Hattori: Yes, in fact, when I passed through the Red Sea it was dark blue.

O: In Turkey, we call the Mediterranean the White Sea. This means that black is North, red is South, and white is West. In other words, the Black Sea is the northern sea, and the Red Sea is the southern sea. To the east there is no sea, but if there had been one, it would have been blue.

H: That is interesting. Even in Japan, since the period of the ancient mound tombs, directions have been designated by colors, as can be seen on the mural paintings in the tombs of Takamatsu south of Nara: Black *Genbu*[19] in the North, Blue Dragon in the East, Red Phoenix in the South, and White Tiger in the West. I think that in continental China this was already the case in the Han period (200 B.C. —A.D. 200), but it must have been introduced to Japan via the Korean peninsula in the Yamato period (300—710 A.D.).

O: Look at the Genbu. The character for the syllable *Gen* is also pronounced *kuro* (black), exactly the old *kara*. *Kara* is the most important word. It is black and at the same time, it means the heavens or the source of the universe. In its Chinese pronunciation, *Yüan,* it was the word applied to the period of Mongolian supremacy. The sky is black.

§

Then there flashed in my brain the description by Stein of a sandstorm in Taklimakan. Midday becomes dark as night. The manes of the horses stream like a madwoman's hair, and the caravan disappears in the dust of the storm. Taklimakan, in the native Uygur language means, "Once a man goes in, he never comes out." (I translated this, "Desert of No Return" in connection with the Marilyn Monroe movie. To my astonishment, the phrasing was stolen for use without my permission in an English-language magazine some months later.)

A black sky—this is not the alpine sky that is so clear and becomes dark so you can see the stars in midday. This sky is a horrible sky. That is why much sorcery originated here, as well as prayers to Heaven and attempts to discern the will of Heaven. And the one whom Heaven chooses is the emperor. When Heaven gets angry, the emperor must be replaced. So a new dynasty is born.

§

In connection with the black sky, I'm thinking of Qin Shuang Di, the First Emperor of the Qin Dynasty (221—206 B.C.). Qin Shuang Di is the emperor who unified China for the first time, but he perpetrated an outrage called the "burning of the books and the act of burying scholars in a pit." These actions caused a dark shadow to fall over his accomplishments: the subjugation of the six eastern kingdoms and the standardization of weights and measures, of money, of the Chinese

---

[19] *Genbu.* An imaginary animal that is a mixture of snake and turtle.

script, and of the nation's laws.   Why did this emperor have 460 scholars buried alive?   Why did he so systematically engage in book burning?

I think this had to do fundamentally with the proper procedure for that ancient "Ceremony for the Achievement of Wisdom" which was to be performed on the top of the sacred Mt. Taishan.   In other words, it concerned this ceremony of the North in which he would receive from Heaven the decree to ascend the emperor's throne.[20]   When he inquired how this ceremony of the sacred mountain worked, the Confucian scholars did not know, could not explain, and could not teach him how to do it.   Qin Shuang Di had no choice but to perform it in his own way.   This event engraved upon his mind the total uselessness of these Confucian scholars.   Since this ceremony was indeed an essential one, he could not forgive their ignorance.

§

Because the emperor has the seal of approval, so to speak, of the universe, this Son of Heaven sits enthroned in the north (*kara*) facing south.   He is looking down Phoenix Street, which starts at the emperor's palace and extends south toward the red Phoenix gate.   In the 13th century when the Mongols ruled China and when Kublai Khan placed the capital in Beijing (which means northern capital), the character pronounced Yüan (source) in Chinese became the Mongols' dynastic name.   This naming is nothing but a confirmation of the concept of "Kara Black = Heaven = Source of Imperial Authority."

This *kara* is construed as having a Mongolian or Turkish origin, and if we trace its etymology, it belonged to the Altaic linguistic family of Siberia and is thought to have spread to the West with the movement of the Turkish people.   At the same time it was transmitted eastward, and spread via the Korean peninsula to the Japanese archipelago.   There are people who say that the Japanese language is unique in the world, but such is not the case.   It is linked to the Turkic or Turkish language[21]

---

[20] The usual term for this in Western histories of China is the Mandate of Heaven.

[21] "Turkish" is a loose synonym for "Turkic," but here we should probably use "Turkic" in the technical sense of the branch of the Altaic family of languages of central and southwest Asia and eastern Europe.   *Random House Dictionary of the English Language.*   Unabridged ed. (1967).

spoken in the Altaic mountain range. Therefore, the two languages are very much the same in structure even today.

Sumo is something that provides evidence for this Altaic route. This ceremonial form of wrestling can be seen in countries along that road: Mongolia, Korea, and Japan. Today the primordial form of the ring has changed and you see a variation. People seem to have forgotten the early features, but originally there were the four pillars near the ring purified by salt, which were an indication of the four directions with their four colors.

Furthermore, the notion of the Heaven-God as it was conceived in Siberia is an instance of shamanism. It is thought that shamanism spread by means of the westward advance of the Turks and Huns from western Turkestan to the northern part of Europe.[22] It also took the road east; shamanism permeated the Korean peninsula, and it went south into the Chinese mainland and also distributed itself throughout the islands of Southeast Asia. It is said to have been introduced into Japan through Kokuryo (a Korean kingdom, 2nd century to the 7th), but whether or not that is true, the fact is clear that Queen Himiko[23] of the

---

[22] Previously in this book Turkmenistan has been referred to. The distinction between Turkestan (a region stretching as a belt across Eurasia) and Turkmenistan (a republic) needs to be emphasized. *Turkestan* is a vast area east of the Caspian Sea encompassing parts of China, Afghanistan, and the Russian region called Turkestan.

[23] Among the fascinating stories about this queen is one that states that when male leaders ("kings") failed to resolve the civil war among their 100 kingdoms, they called on this woman to assume authority as queen; this she did and in that capacity enforced peace for a long period. It is difficult in the English-language histories of Japan to look up this individual because of the several spellings of her name: for example, Pimiku, Pimiko, Himiko, and Himeko. Papinot (p. 748) has this to say (omitting Chinese characters): "*Yametsu-hime*. She is a descendant of Watatsumi and ruled the country of Yame, north of Kyūshū, from 190 to 247. The Chinese and Korean annals give her the name Pimiho which is a corruption of Hime-ko. She conquered the savage tribes of southern Tsukushi and received from the Chinese Emperor Ming-ti a golden seal with the title of king of the country of Wo. [Wa in Japanese] At her death, over 100 of her servants buried themselves alive around her tomb." In the context of the present chapter, it is relevant to point out that the first Chinese character for her country of Yametai is the sacred shamanistic eight. (The second character means woman.) In Japanese "Himiko" probably derives from Hi-no-Miko, honorable child of the sun.

Yamatai Kingdom was a shaman (*miko*, necromancer, medium). In the "Legend of the Wa People," a part of the History of the Three Kingdoms, she is described as the "queen. . . who performs Demoniac Service," that is, magic. In contrast to Buddhism's *nine*, the sacred number of shamanism is *eight*. In proper names such as **O**ya**s**hima (Great Eight Islands, a mythological name for Japan), **Ya**oyorozu-no-Kami (8,000,000 deities), **Ya**mata no orochi (mythological serpent with 8 heads and 8 tails), and **Hachi**man (the god of war), the sacred 8 survives in the Japanese pronunciation *ya* or *hachi*.

§

Since this is the case, you may wonder whether *kara* also has survived in the Japanese language. That is indeed true: Japanese use of *Kara* in the expression *Kara-Tenjiku* (China and India) is surely one instance. (On the Korean peninsula as well, the words pronounced *kara*, *kaya*, and *kan* all stem from *kara*). *Kara* is used in several Japanese compounds such as *karaori* (Chinese fabric), *karakami* (the thick paper used in sliding doors in Japan), and in *karatsu* (chinaware) when people talk about porcelain in Kansai (the area encompassing Kyoto, Osaka, and Kobe). This word *kara* carries the double nuance of imported goods and superior quality. Before Sen-no-Rikyu (1520—1591) established the tea ceremony,[24] the tea parties of Sakai[25] were the mundane meetings of appreciation for *karamono*, goods from abroad including Western countries.

As can be seen in the *Shōsōin*, many superb art products of China, along with religious thoughts, were introduced into Japan during the Tang period (618-907). It is also true that in the succeeding periods of Sung, Yüan (Mongol), Ming, and Ch'ing (Manchu) ending in 1912, various Chinese articles were imported. Nevertheless, the Japanese call

---

Hence, according to a note by Hattori, "she could be assimilated to Amaterasu, goddess of the sun."

[24] *Sen-no-Rikyu* was also known as Sen Rikyu and Sōeki. *Cha-no-yu*, the tea ceremony he founded, included the art of flower arranging and provided a way of perfecting the self in serenity and so escaping the tyranny of mundane affairs.

[25] Sakai, south of Osaka, was at this time a center of commerce. According to Papinot, it was the principal port of Japan throughout the medieval period. Foreign ships came here.

these articles as a whole group, *kara,* an Altai word (not a Tang Chinese word).[26]

On the one hand, "West" is the direction of the Pure Land or Western Paradise (*Jōdo*). In Europe, from time immemorial the phrase has been "light from the East," but in that same East people were looking westward for the Pure Land. The West is white, and in the expressions *Byaku-Roji* (white route), *Byaku-Ren* (white lotus), and *Byakkō* (white light) are heard echoes of the "pure." The Pure Land of Amitabha lies in the West. Furthermore, the Buddha of the future is Bodhisattva Maitreya (Miroku in Japanese) who must also manifest himself from the West. He is similar to Christ who appears at the end of the world. Also, the legend of a "Queen Mother of the West" (Xi Wang Mu) told from ancient times in China is consistent with this same idea. She was a fairy in paradise who is supposed to live beyond deserts and mountains in the West.

§

An interesting fact is that this kind of orientation of values by directions completely changes the maps within oriental human consciousness. In the 7th century, Xuen Zhang, who left Ch'ang-an on a journey to seek out original Buddhist sutras, did head west as viewed from his starting point of Ch'ang-an, but from Sogdiana[27] he goes south to Gandhara (the area of northwest Pakistan and eastern Afghanistan) and to the Indus River area. Extending his journey from there to the mouth of the Ganges, he proceeds southeast. Nevertheless, the name of the record of his trip is, "An Account of a Journey to the West." In the T'ongdosa monastery in the Kyonju area of Korea, the map which records the great Tang westward journey by this Xuen Zhang is preserved, but on the scroll as viewed from right to left Eurasia looks flat. We find India to the west of China and Sri Lanka to the west of India. And, again, farther west is depicted Kunlun Shan, which is a Chinese Utopia at ocean's end. Once in Venice I had the experience of viewing a map of a flat world such as this, but with the Mediterranean Sea as the center.

---

[26] Matters related to *kara* are richly embedded in the game of go and in the traditions and practices accompanying it. Go also has a cosmic dimension involving the stars.

[27] *Sogdiana.* A province of the ancient Persian Empire. Compare with modern Uzbekistan (Samarkand its capital).

In regard to the Chinese continent and the Korean peninsula, from ancient to medieval times, and even right up into the early modern period, it was a common idea that China was above; Korea, in the middle; and Japan, below. Consequently, until the Ming Dynasty (1368—1644), on maps made in China or Korea, the Japanese archipelago was shown to be in the South China Sea.   In extreme cases, it was placed closer to the South Pole, with Kyushu in the North and Honshu's city of Aomori, which is actually situated at its northern tip, at the South on the map—a complete turn-around. On such a map Japan looks like a hanging salmon. We cannot explain this simply as due to a lack of surveying techniques. We must understand that North was the direction of authority and excellence; in other words, it was *kara* from which travellers go down to the southern regions of barbarity.

Even in the discussions about the legendary kingdom of Yamatai (Japan about third century), many fail to recognize the fact that the ancient maps were the product of culturally conditioned consciousness. I feel that many people are discussing these matters with only modern maps in their minds. Since modern maps did not exist, such discussion gives rise to many useless doubts and misunderstandings. When the "History of the Wei Dynasty" speaks of "x days by ship to the South," that actually means to the East or Northeast in today's geography. The phrase "waterway to the south" is not just a mistake in writing, but means "by ship to the south," really east, if one imagines an old map and agrees to take into account some of the map's assumptions. Thus, starting from northern Kyushu, if they go "south" on the Inland Sea, they arrive at Yamato (now the region of Nara), and, if they go "south" by way of the Sea of Japan, they arrive at Izumo. This road that I was retracing on the Ark of Peace was the very one which brought the idea of Heaven = God to the Japanese archipelago.

On March 3 of 1991, our ship was heading quietly for Osaka's harbor, a full moon was reflected in the Inland Sea. It was the end of the 145-day voyage from Venice. As I stood alone on the foredeck at 1 a.m., islands were coming in sight like silhouettes in the moonlight. They were wrapped in silent, endless silver waves. Those silver waves grew dim as I forgot to wipe away the tears that were trickling down from my eyes.

Part II. Dialogue Between Civilizations

Letter 7

Reorienting the Cultural World Order

Dear Friend,

Standing at the dawn of a new year, I am thinking of the skies of faraway Japan. As you know, European skies in winter are dark and cold, as if they symbolize that for a number of years world history has been too severely darkened and distorted to allow the unclouded sun to shine through.

A New World Order is a concept of a world in the process of revision and reconstruction that has been talked about for many years. It doesn't mean the "New World Order" that America began to speak of after the collapse of the old Soviet Union. At first it was a way of thinking of the New World Economic Order adopted by the United Nations in the 70's, and from that was born the conception called the New Information Order which was supposed to correct the qualitative and quantitative gaps among nations as well as the one-way flow of information around the world. However, I consider that *culture* must certainly be a central problem in the 21st century. It could be called the challenge of a "new world cultural order."

It has been pointed out again and again that, at the root of almost all the disputes of humanity, lies the ever-increasing disparity between the rich and the poor. The income differential between the presently developing nations and the more secure advanced nations has been increasing. In the Middle Ages the ratio of rich to poor was probably 1 to 3. At present the number has become 1 to 15 or even 1 to 30. Although there have been some exceptions in the newly industrialized nations of Southeast Asia and in the oil producing nations, there is a tendency for the further growth in this disparity to go on apace. The Third World feels extreme impatience with this. The rise of a common feeling among the more than one hundred Non-Aligned Nations reflects nothing less than this intense impatience.

To say, "Economic development is nothing but the result of the effort of a people; any lag in growth is that people's responsibility," is an absurd remark. Not only does it reflect ignorance of the structure of the present world economy, it also fails to recognize the vast scars left over from colonialism. Colonialism means economic exploitation and robbery, such as shown by the East India companies that received many hundreds of times of return on their relatively small investments, or the purchase of Manhattan Island from the Indians for some round beads and a knife worth about $24. It is also a history of slaughter and destruction as seen in the examples of the Aztec and Inca civilizations. Furthermore, it is the history of human enslavement, of which the remaining scars are visible even today on the Ivory Coast and on the Senegalese Gorée Island. Were it not for colonialism, the empire of Mali would probably have continued to exist in Africa, and two of the colonial countries of Indochina—Cambodia and Vietnam—would not have met with their recent tragedies.

Friend, I spoke just now of "human enslavement." I did not say, "slave trading" because I wanted to mention the more universal enslavement of mind and spirit experienced by great numbers of people. It is not just the fact of trade in human beings. Human enslavement involves far more than the economic factor alone. We may, with even more justice, call it the greatest crime committed by colonialism. It was the "enslavement of the spirit" in the colonized nations.

How many colonial peoples and nations have lost their own languages! Or else their own languages are regarded as "second languages." In such cases, they must encounter a death of the inner spirit, or of what Americans call spunk. A language is itself a culture, and we must recognize culture as a system of values. When one value system rules another value system, then that brings about a complete master-servant relationship between the two nations or peoples, and the master will never try to appreciate the servant on equal terms.

I recall the conversation I once had with a scholar from Morocco, published by *Le Monde* (the French newspaper). He said, "The New World Economic Order was a 'stillborn baby' . . . All our efforts collided with a cultural barrier, and we cannot get past it . . . ."

Culture indeed is a people's soul. It is their dignity, their very existence or being. It is solely by means of culture that a people possesses sovereignty.

"The ability of Poland, during the ordeal of two world wars, to maintain its national sovereignty in spite of being dismembered and occupied, depended solely on its culture." These are the words uttered in June of 1979 by Pope John Paul II on the occasion of his visit to UNESCO. Colonialism has stolen this sovereignty from many nations and peoples—by *education*. And whenever sovereignty is lost, then at that very moment genuine dialogue becomes nonexistent. This is how I would unravel the meaning of "cultural barriers."

§

A culture originally enriches itself by *encountering* other cultures; such meetings will create new and revitalized traditions. Often the word "traditional" is used as though it were synonymous with "past" or "bygone," but I think tradition is something that must be very much alive in the *here and now*. Even if we think of modern France as the synonym of culture, we should realize that its culture does not remain just as it was in ancient Gaul. No culture remains throughout time just as it was. Because of its geographical setting, French culture through the ages has encountered many highly heterogeneous cultures. Out of those encounters a new cultural synthesis has emerged which is the result of a compilation of cultures.

The same situation exists in Japan. The nation has absorbed everything into the special nurturing medium called the Japanese language and in the process has created its traditional culture in an ever-expanding form. Even the modernization of this nation since the Meiji Restoration in 1868 is not a phenomenon outside this framework. That, too, was due to cultural encounter, and what largely happened is the "Japanization of what was imported from the West" rather than the "Westernization of Japan"—exactly like the earlier Japanization of Buddhism when it was brought over from the Chinese continent.

However, when the master-servant relationship is established, the effect is that the one culture erases the other. What then emerges is a world ruled by the law of the jungle. There is no sadder state of affairs than a subjugation of spirit in which one learns to depreciate one's own culture.

The problem is that, even after former colonies got their independence in the 1960's, the aftereffects of colonialism remained as of old and threw large shadows on those countries' true independence. Much unchanged education is being conducted under the name of "technical cooperation" in former colonies and is contributing unconsciously to maintaining the old master-slave subordination. What makes this harder to identify and cope with is that technical collaborators from foreign countries are almost always full of good intentions. This kind of movement is called the *new colonialism*. The expressions "cultural aggression" and "educational aggression" have been coined for it. However, the voices of protest have not yet become loud enough or numerous enough to evoke an international cry for reform.

What is necessary now is the reform of consciousness. Asians and Africans should hold their heads high in cultural identities that are their own. Any look of secret contempt or lack of understanding must disappear from the eyes of outside collaborators "full of good intentions." That will involve a reform of consciousness including not only those in the developing countries but everyone. Toward that end what must be done? Here I would like to mention the most basic thing. It is to understand that the image of world culture has hitherto contained a "warp." This "cultural warp" urgently needs correction. The need exists not at the level of specialized books but at the level of schoolbooks.

This warping has arisen from the fact that the history of world cultures has been written according to one viewpoint. Moreover, such cultural history is contained in any textbook of world history that has as its keynotes economics and military affairs; hence it is written as if cultural values are directly proportional to power relations. That is the viewpoint of Western Europe. It is, moreover, the viewpoint that learned the so-called perspective method born in the Renaissance. Accordingly, the structure of cultures in Hellenism and Christianity is made into a large close-up, and the cultural sphere outside the West has a much smaller and far more blurred existence. The world vision displayed on this distorted map uses the measures of material civilization inspired by natural science to evaluate the cultural values of other civilizations.

The problem is that this cultural image, which played a leading part in European thinking, entered the textbooks and has been distributed throughout the whole world since the colonial era. Japan is no exception because it strove to introduce translations of many Western works. As a result, new textbooks, such as those on Japanese history, had to be created—just as if Japan were outside world history. And even now worship of the West is still alive. Hiding at the bottom of such worship are its counterparts: discrimination, segregation, and ignorance of the people of Arabian, Asian, and African civilizations.

Here I would like to note what was done consciously or unconsciously to erase entire pages from the world's cultural history. For example, the Italian Renaissance was a revival of ancient Greece, and it was also the period during which Chinese arts were being imported. But this second point is not written about. It is as though there were something shameful about Europe's learning anything from a backwards country such as China. While many pages are devoted to the history of Rome, the histories of Luoyang (Lo-yang) and Ch'ang-an[28], two cities of equal importance to Rome in their sphere, are not written about. In Ch'ang-an during the 8th-century Tang period, there was an influx from Japan of more than 2,000 overseas students, and the city states sending diplomatic missions to China amounted to 300. Now Japanese learn of Caesar but ignore Gao Zong (third emperor of the Tang dynasty).[29] In fact, the Chinese influence of this period was so great that not only did it affect the planning of the Japanese cities of Nara and Kyoto but also all present-day university terminology such as "*kyōju*" (professor) and "*gakushi*" (bachelor). These terms used in the universities in Luoyang were introduced throughout Japan.

Another wonderful example is the fact that people all over the world, including Indians and Arabs, are taught that the 15th century is the period of explorers and discoveries. Why in the world do people, who have even older civilizations than Western Europe, need to be "discovered"? There are also many factual mistakes involved. The following example is pertinent whether one lives in America or India. Apart from whether America was discovered before Columbus by the Vikings, when we speak about precursors of great navigation, we must first cite the extraordinary expeditions of Zheng He (Cheng Ho) as the beginning of the Age of Great voyages. His voyages totaled seven round trips, beginning in 1405 and involving several hundred great

---

[28] *Luoyang and Ch'ang-an.* *Luoyang* is important as the capital of several ruling dynasties and as a Buddhist center. Famous Buddhist caves were constructed south of the city by imperial order. *Ch'ang-an* (Xian) in the Tang period was equivalent to Rome at its peak when we look at cultural, commercial, scientific, even military influence. The capital was shifted back and forth between these two cities.

[29] Gao Zong, also known as Kao-tsung or Li Chih, expanded the Tang empire to encompass Korea.

ships and tens of thousands of sailors. Starting from Canton, he led these expeditions to cross through the Malaccan Straits, to proceed from the Indian Ocean to the Persian Gulf, and to extend as far as the east coast of Africa. He was pioneering in global navigation eighty-seven years before Columbus was seeking India, China, and Zipangu (the country of gold, Japan)[30] and ninety-three years before Vasco da Gama's discovery of the Cape of Good Hope. In the case of da Gama, we need to note that the Arabian who was his pilot already knew the sea route that he was showing to da Gama. That man's name, as we saw in Letter 3, is Ahmed bin Majid.

When we look at the history of cultural interchange, we do see a huge amount of East-West cultural interchange, which started about A.D. 1, reached a climax in the 8th century, and has been continuing since then. The chief actors on the sea route were the Chinese, Indians, and Arabians, while on the overland silk route, they were the Persians and Chinese. That interchange linked Greece and the Orient, and it sent oriental handicrafts to Europe and Africa. The Romans themselves went to far-away East Asia. When I reflect on such things, I must say that to speak of the "discovery" voyages of the 15th century or of new continents "discovered" for the first time by Europeans during that century sounds really strange.

Friend, did you ever consider how to solve this strange puzzle? I think that, in fact, just as there had been isolation in Japan, so also there had been isolation in Western Europe. The explanation stems from the fact of the "crescent battle formation of Islam"[31] referring to the power and influence of Islam from the 8th century to the 16th. From modern Turkey to the Persian Gulf, on both banks of the Red Sea, the crescent that spread throughout all of North Africa to the Iberian Peninsula almost encircled Europe. With the frigid Arctic Circle to the north and nothing but ocean to the west, Europe was thus isolated for several centuries. Consequently, for Europe the "discovery" of the East at the end of the 15th century, must be said to have been, in fact, a

---

[30] For the sake of completeness, we should explain that Columbus had been inspired by Marco Polo's book to try to find these countries. He was not seeking spices but gold.—E.H.

[31] The "crescent battle formation" is a poetic expression meaning that Islam surrounded Europe in the form of a crescent.

"rediscovery," but this word was mistakenly left out of the history textbooks written after the opening of the colonial period.[32]

I have spoken of "mistakes." But were they really mistakes? Even if Europeans experienced a period of isolation in their region, any European historian should have learned that these same Muslims who encircled Europe were carrying on trade by land and sea routes and were also making significant advances in science and technology. The Crusades of Christendom ended in military and religious failure, but because of the cultural interaction with Islam, important innovations were introduced in architectural techniques, mathematics, chemistry, and natural science. Why are those things not written down more clearly and distinctly in the West?

Surely there are persons studying philosophy who must be aware that the complete works of Aristotle were preserved in an Arabic translation without which they would not have been transmitted to the present. A well-informed student of philosophy would also be aware that the modern philosophies of Descartes and Kant are developments or antitheses of the scholastic philosophy of St. Thomas Aquinas who was himself indebted to the Arabic versions translated into Latin for his own introduction to Aristotle, without which his own philosophy would have been impossible.

I cannot help but think that in cultural history the full story of this significant Islamic contribution to human civilization has been *intentionally* erased. If that is so, we must find the cause for such intentional omissions in the deep scars, grudges, and enmity left by what are called religious wars. Zheng He, mentioned earlier, planned to go to Mecca on one of his voyages to fulfill his duty as a Moslem. Might this fact help explain the elimination of his name from history? I must add that Western histories had a similar purpose to the first Japanese history, the 8th-century A.D. *Kojiki*. Its purpose was to justify the government of the time. [33]

---

[32] Serious matters deserve serious treatment, but sometimes humor relaxes and clarifies. An American bumper sticker reads: "In 1492 the Indians discovered Columbus lost at sea."

[33] More specifically, the *Kojiki* was written by the Fujiwara clan to legitimize the imperial court by showing them to be descendants from the sun goddess, Amaterasu, and at the same time to give the raison d'etre of the Fujiwara family as her minister.

Now is the time for a universal human history to be written. It would seek to transcend ethnocentricity. Such a history should have an equitable viewpoint that respects the dignity of many cultures. Presupposing a rational approach, it should extol many virtues: esteem for life, harmony with nature, courtesy and respect, serenity, and compassion.[34] In that way, the peoples of the world can escape the yoke of present-day hatreds and grudge-bearing and may be allowed and encouraged to take a new step forward.

Once André Malraux said to me, "The 21st century must become the century of global culture." He explained to me that the 20th century was one of war, as the 19th had been one of progress, but I feel he had a premonition that this new cultural order was necessary for the very *existence* of human beings.

---

[34] This last, *benevolence* or *compassion* in Japanese, encompasses the Buddhist virtues of active benevolence, universal love, and loving-kindness. In these respects, it overlaps with the meaning of a Greek term for divine love, *Agapé*, which occupies the apex in the Christian hierarchy of values. There is also an equivalent to this concept in the Hebrew Bible, *hesed*, usually translated "loving-kindness" or "steadfast love."

Letter 8

Western Logic and Dialogue

Dear Friend,

How many years has it been since Arimasa Mori passed away in Paris? However long it has been since we were separated from him, it seems only yesterday. Time slips by so fast.

I was on stage with Professor Mori in Paris just ten days before he sustained a fall. On that day he spoke to high school students sent by the National Federation of UNESCO Associations of Japan. The theme of his speech was supposed to be European culture in the light of his experiences during a long stay in Europe, but at that time he spoke solely about language.

Afterwards I escorted Mori to his house on Rue Grand Degré in the vicinity of Notre Dame. When we parted he said, "After I return from a demanding lecture trip to Japan in the fall, let's get together again," but that was the last time we met. Later when I thought about it, I felt that in the somewhat impatient tone he showed at the time of that lecture, he was hiding a deep tiredness. However, let us now return to the talk itself. I wish to give attention to the fact that such a great thinker as Arimasa Mori occupied the extreme situation for a philosopher of having to leave the problem of language unsolved. Mori spoke as follows on what is called the difficulty of a foreign language: "Reading is easy. Writing also is easy. You can even speak if you exert yourself. However, listening is difficult."

In other words, the problem of *reading* a foreign language is at one's own pace. If you don't understand, you can reread the passage or if you still don't understand you can even stop reading. As for *writing* in the language, this is possible, for this also is a problem of studying by oneself, and, therefore, of constructing one's own sentences. There are also people who say speaking another language is difficult, but it is basically the same as writing it, since what one wants to say is something one already knows and can practice. However, what is called *listening* is difficult. The reason is that since whatever the other party wants to say is not known by us beforehand, it is not a problem of hearing alone. Understanding the other party is truly difficult. That is the main sense of what Mori said at that time. Perhaps the point was not quite clear to Japanese high school students, but to me who had lived a long time in Europe it was very understandable. What Mori was speaking of here was what might be termed "the chatting logic"[35] that forms the foundation of European culture.

§

This kind of spoken logic is said to have been constructed in the beginning by free citizens who at their leisure gathered for discussion and debate in the agora, the public square of Athens. Such conversation became the foundation of what eventually spread through many centuries and throughout the countries of Europe as dialogue. Dialogue does not arise unless at least two people are involved. Moreover, like tennis, if the opponent does not return the ball hit from this side, the game of dialogue comes to a halt. In order for it to be a good game, the ball must be returned energetically and in an unexpected way.

To say that Logos is supposed to be ONE is the interpretation later arising from the influence of Christianity. At the time of its origin in Greece, Logos had a more plural meaning and usage; like conversation

---

[35] Here and in what follows, "logic" and "chatting logic" will carry one part of the meaning of the Greek word *logos*, namely, the combination of reason and talk that produces rational discourse. When the formal structure of reasoned thinking and speaking is stressed in modern English usage, Logos is expressed as "logic." When the speaking side is stressed, the word "dialogue" sometimes is used. Both words stem etymologically from *logos*. Their meanings in English might be fused into "logical dialogue" or "reasonable conversation," neither of which does justice to the Japanese expression *shaberu ronri* (talking logic, chatting logic, or chattering logic). The context shows that "chatting logic" is perhaps the closest equivalent, since a good-humored critique of Western modes of wordy, and sometimes too combative, discussion is clearly intended.

it consisted of many words. Yet, one might argue, there is one truth (Logos in its later sense) as the basis of any conversation that goes anywhere. What the Greeks first experienced was many sparks of Logos fighting each other.[36] Among those "sparks" are items that emanate from what is shared or held in common, *homologeima*.[37] However, when two *logoi* (the Greek plural of Logos) remain in opposition, the resulting war of words lacks any common ground. Then only an implausible miracle such as a *deus ex machina* in a stage comedy by Aristophanes can bring discussion to the point of agreement or accord. In this case, chatting logic becomes a trivial game in which the *logoi* are too pluralized and divided.

Once, when I was in Greece, I observed a group of elderly people, their chairs arranged in a circle, chattering all day in a park. I was impressed by the Greek tradition of the agora. This chatting logic travelled north with Caesar. It left us many theological theories as a result of seminars conducted in Latin. (Both St. Augustine and St. Thomas used chatting logic in their seminars.) And since Descartes, this "logic" reached its peak in a perfect language called French.

In this connection I recall a visit I once had with the editor of the *Le Monde* paper. When I inquired, "Why does your newspaper not use photographs," his answer was certainly explicit: "The French language has developed to such a point of perfection that it can express anything."

Friend, can we live in such a world as the editor imagines? In that world, not only must you use a perfect language, you must principally remember that in communication, what you want to express will require twice your usual effort if it is to succeed. For communication to be truly superb in the occidental world, everything should be expressed correctly, and, in such a world, there is nothing that cannot be expressed. "I cannot express it" should, in fact, be taken to mean "I have no idea."[38] You must have ears to hear the Logos (intention and

---

[36] Speaking more metaphysically, one might say, "The Word shoots out words—and other things."

[37] This Greek word, as used by Plato and others, concerns what is agreed upon, taken for granted, or a postulate of reasoning.

[38] In the Japanese version of this book, I was ironic in what I quoted from the French editor but, writing in Japanese style, I chose to remain modest enough not to criticize him. Yet I did, and do, feel free to bring out some of the

meaning) of your partner. If you do not have such ears, then your conversation will not be dialogue but only monologue.

For example, in 1968 at the time of the university collective bargaining conflict in Japan, there was certainly a lot of monologue. By contrast, even in the middle of the French upheaval where the spark of student protest had started spreading worldwide, it was possible to form a *comité paritaire* (committee of equality) to create a situation for dialogue. The very tradition of true dialogue became a primary factor in the achievement of university reform. Here, when one's own language (Logos) attains common points with the other party, the discussion for once ends with the words, *Vous avez raison* (You have reason, *Logos*—you are right) or *Nous sommes d'accord* (We've reached common ground).

In contrast to this, the Japanese style of *Logos* has been the principle of *no reason* or even *unreasoning reason*. It's a world of lack of confidence in the written word (with the meaning sought between the lines of printed characters) and of communication from soul to soul. If we are to use coarser language, we might call it gut feeling, or, more politely, heart-to-heart communication, or even communication by force of personality. During the university disturbances in Japan, people only imitated dialogue. In a place where there is no tradition of dialogue, efforts at collective bargaining have been unsuccessful.

In Japan what is called self-expression is not easy. Even if some kind of expression is possible, there is an unspoken understanding that whatever is attempted by means of *Logos* is not the final act because what is most important is invisible and cannot be expressed. That is because the truth that the Japanese are seeking is always a matter of ethical relationship or harmony. Greek *pathos* (feeling or empathy) is always given a higher rating than Logos or logical reasoning.

§

As Isaiah Ben-Dasan[39] once indicated, Onda Moku the feudal overseer who appears in the ancient book *Higurashi-Suguri,* acted like

---

consequences of too much confidence in language generally or in one's own "perfect" language, specifically.—E.H

[39]*Isaiah Ben-Dasan.* Pseudonym for a Japanese editor named Yamamoto who preferred to remain anonymous when he published his book. It became somewhat of a sensation in Japan and was subsequently published in English (Weatherhill, 1981) as *The Japanese and the Jews.*

a typical Japanese. I think it is interesting, in fact, that, using the Japanese approach, he pacified the peasants who had started a riot. Viewed from the point of view of Western logic, his arbitration was unfair since he did not grant their petition. However, in the end the peasants were moved to tears and went peacefully to their homes.

How could such a thing have been possible? At the beginning Moku anticipates the peasants' claims and, after stating them to the peasants, says, "You are right in claiming these things," (in other words, there is a reason for saying such a thing) "but . . ."[40] Then he states the contrary which is his own position of refusal. Surprisingly for Westerners, this means a true beginning has taken place just where a Western dialogue might have ended. For the Japanese sincerity is more important than reason.

Requiring our notice here are the following matters. (1) The Japanese mind does not deny *Logos*. (2) That same mind handles Logos and Pathos at an identical site in the brain. According to Tadanobu Tsunoda, that must be the left hemisphere of the brain.[41]

Knocking the "ball" of conversation back and forth using only the left brain became especially embarrassing to me, a Japanese going out into international society. A while ago I compared that to a game, one that is born where there is *leisure*, and one with *rules*. Consequently, it is possible for two European friends to have a serious quarrel, and after

---

[40]In Japanese, *saredo,* an old samurai expression.

[41]It is classic brain theory to say that the right hemisphere treats art, imagination, intuition, and feeling by *pathos,* while the left hemisphere treats logic and mathematics. Dr. Tsunoda, a medical doctor with a specialty in severe ear problems, found that certain sounds which are caught by the right brains of Americans and residents of Eurasia (even Koreans) are processed by the left hemisphere in the case of Japanese. Examples of such sounds include the singing of the wind in the pine trees, the rippling of a river, and songs of insects. By means of his laboratory tests, Tsunoda has found that the wave patterns of these sounds are identical with the wave patterns of spoken vowels. He concludes that the omnipresence of vowels in Japanese has created the unique Japanese brain in which the left hemisphere treats not only logic but also some feelings. Thus it is heart instead of pure reason. If a Japanese lived a long time in the Western world, as I did, that person's left brain could become so fatigued by logic that he or she might lose the Japanese soul. That thought is shocking!—E.H.

the argument they can be friends again.　During such a quarrel, Japanese will be anxious. Later they will be surprised at the amicable outcome. At such a time, Japanese are dominated by the strong feeling of wanting to avoid hurting their friend. So they tend to say yes easily or, if they know French "*Oui, c'est ça,*" which is not always the answer in their mind. A discussion that ought to become pleasant completely stops at that point. It is like the famous and aggressive tennis star Agassi playing with an elementary school boy. The ball is never returned. For the Westerner, a Japanese is nothing but a helpless opponent in discussion.

Again, how to construct a discussion is difficult. One must have wit and esprit de corps. The rules of discussion must be clearly delineated. Thirty years ago when I was studying in Paris, the thing I most admired when invited into a French home is illustrated by the saying, "The core of hospitality is conversation." The duty of a French hostess was especially difficult because she was coordinating topics while showing concern for each guest. But her own way of speaking was so beautiful that I felt as if I was watching the placement of flowers in ikebana. Such an accomplishment is really an ikebana of words, since the words are examined and selected one by one and the main lines of discussion drawn out clearly. Along with that goes the fact of arranging the whole with beautiful simplicity and compactness. Just as a Japanese housewife selectively arranges flowers in her parlor, so the French lady was offering guests her ikebana of words. The only difference is that the ikebana of words involves the logic (or rules) of dialogue, and so is not complete with one offering of words, though ikebana is done with one set of flowers. Each guest must add auxiliary branches to the main lines of classical ikebana depicting heaven, earth, and humanity. That addition becomes your table duty; for the sake of beauty, the joint work of those who converse must never add an auxiliary branch that is too similar to one already in place. For the sake of dialogue as a joint conversational project, the words "Yes, that's right" signal conversational failure.

§

Arimasa Mori while lecturing in the Japanese Embassy in Paris once defined the Japanese people this way: "The Japanese are the human beings who speak a special language called Japanese." To extend his comment, we may say that being Japanese means having a brain that is so constructed and organized that it has to think in the special language called Japanese. Later in this same session, Arimasa Mori referred to the Japanese as having a unique binary relationship to each other.

"I" is not an independent I. It is "you" from the point of view of the other. Consequently, depending on who the other is, the "I" changes to *boku, ore, temae, watakushi,* etc. The "you" also changes— it changes to *kisama, omae, kimi, anata,* etc. The host (I) and the guest (you) are understood and defined by the binary relationship; in fact, they find their identities in a given place and time.

To whatever extent we Japanese live in our language, to that extent our feelings and logic are processed on the same side of our brains. So we say first, "*Hai*" or "Yes." This *hai* means nothing but, "I see" (or perhaps, "I'm being friendly"). It has nothing to do with "yes" or "no" as expressions of our own private opinion. This would naturally occasion misunderstanding for a non-Japanese, wouldn't it?

§

The office of the director of the Japanese *Maison du Japon* (House of Japan) is located in the *Cité Universitaire,* a huge campus which is part of the University of Paris where more than fifty countries have their own homes for students. This *Maison* was furnished with an old 17th century pipe organ, a beautifully simple instrument totally lacking useless decoration. Because for many years owning the organ had been the desire of Professor Mori's heart, I think he used his salary as Director of the House to buy the organ. One evening I was invited by Mori to be his only supper guest. Before supper (which he almost forgot!) he played Bach and Palestrina for me for three long hours. He played as one in meditation or as if he were melting into the music.

France admitted Arimasa Mori into its country but did not fully accept him into its culture. It tended to ostracize outsiders, so he was driven deep into his own private world of feeling. Mori fought for thirty years to be able to melt into this portion of Western civilization. And even for Mori who mastered French, the result of his search was to understand that at the core of an alien civilization is its language. In the strains of Mori's organ music, Notre Dame Cathedral, the symbol of French civilization, was at first far away as he tried to reach it, then drew nearer, and finally leaves him alone again, disappearing totally from his sight.[42] In the horrific twilight of his last days, I think he was able to find a tranquillity of mind solely in music that transcends language.

---

[42] "Notre Dame far away" and "Notre Dame disappearing" are two of Mori's book titles. Mori was born into a Christian family.—E.H.

Letter 9

Invisible War

Dear Friend,

I wrote you a little while ago trying to elucidate a "warp in our cultural images," a warp that permeates not only the Western world but every corner of the modern world. In the same context I wrote of how I saw emerging as our central challenge "a new world order." To my surprise, not long after that, something quite similar was published by Seuil Press: *Promesses de l'Islam* ("The Promises of Islam") by Roger Garaudy.[43]

"There will be no new world economic order without a new world cultural order." Garaudy continues, "The dialogue of civilizations has become a necessity, urgent and unimpeachable. It is the problem of humanity's survival."

Of course, it is natural for someone of Garaudy's cultural background to write as one for whom Islamic culture is central, but this book on its first page begins with a shocking phrase, "The Occident is an accident." The book created a sensation among many persons who think about culture. The outline of what Garaudy, a respected scholar, argues is the following:

The Occident, by claiming as its origin or heritage only two sources, i.e., the Greco-Roman and Judeo-Christian, has suppressed intentionally the cultural influence of the Orient and Africa. It is as though a child who has made good must, in order to enhance his own "greatness," pretend to be an orphan or deny at least one of his parents. In the present case, this involves denying what Garaudy calls the "third legacy," by which he refers to what Islam has contributed intellectually

---

[43] Garaudy is a Frenchman who converted to Islam.

and scientifically to European civilization since the 8th century. This denial has been constant and clear since the 13th century and is an occidental crime. Moreover, this same Western Civilization that shows increasing arrogance has even come to the point of forcing on the world its own concept of "progress."

Garaudy, whose past career includes having been dismissed from the French Communist Party, at this point severely denounces both the capitalist and socialist systems as birds of a feather or, as we say in Japanese, occupants of the same badger's den. Concerning socialism, he criticizes especially the fact that it aims for the same economic growth (and growth indicators) as Western European capitalism. Both systems have become oppressors of the people, exploiters of the Third World, and partners and rivals in both hegemony and the fearful arms race.

His severe denunciation of the concept of Progress is apparent in his words in his *Appel aux Vivants* ("A Call to Survivors") where he discusses the concept of leaving people to their own fate in the midst of unrestricted competition[44] as the formula for "progress." Garaudy also states most frankly that European culture had entered a blind alley of its own making. He writes, "Word usage reflects the disintegration of the West. Peace is now called 'a balance of terror.' The betrayal of people by the state is called 'national security.' Institutional or governmental violence is called 'order.' The competition of the jungle is called 'liberalism',"[45] and an ensemble of all these is called "progress."

Roger Garaudy concludes that the concept of Western progress will lead the human race to its death. And he explains that Westerners must rediscover two ideas that are living and breathing in the midst of this "third legacy," the ideas of "transcendence" and "community." Garaudy proceeds to look again at the world of Sufism as has Michel Random who wrote *Maulana*. This we can say is a type of severe criticism of the West by Westerners, but if we change the point of view, the fact of this kind of self-criticism shows the possibility of salvation for the West.

---

[44] Compare the English proverb, "Every man for himself, and the devil take the hindmost."

[45] What Garaudy calls "liberalism" would probably, in America, be called "libertarianism."

§

In some contrast, V. S. Naipaul in his recent *The Twilight of Islam* has preferred to take up the problem of every Islamic people that aims to return to its purity, especially through revolution. Naipaul, born of Indian parents in Trinidad and Tobago,[46] has been in the running for a Nobel prize as an English-language author. I think his success depends on his experiential style of writing and his pointed insights.

On the one hand, there are the West's endeavors to minimize Islamic elements within its own heritage. On the other hand, the majority of Islamic nations, as has become obvious since the Iranian Revolution, have sought to exclude all elements of other cultures (here, of course, the subject is Western cultures). Advocates of Islamic purity are trying to discover their cultural identity by returning to the world of the Koran. These antagonistic tendencies—to ignore Islamic contributions in the West and to eliminate Western elements in the Islamic sphere— now cover much of the globe.

On an emotional level I can understand this new emphasis on Islamic fundamentalism as an effort to get rid of colonial subordination and its aftereffects since the 16th century. This movement to achieve Islamic purity is also the reason for the formation of ALECSO (Arab League Educational, Cultural, and Scientific Organization), which could be called an Arab version of UNESCO. That is not an action but a reaction, and internationally it should be received as a just demand for a reinstatement of status or a restitution of what has been neglected by history.

My friend, nevertheless, as I earlier wrote, "Culture essentially enriches itself by encounters," and if you've also learned à la Garaudy that "civilizations, by their encounters, may conceive a child," then won't you also know that any civilization without a "child" will by and by grow old and die without issue. Hence, we must be aware that the "dialogue of civilizations" is necessary for the survival of one's own civilization, and not just for that of all the others.

By the way, this kind of *dialogue*, as I wrote you last time, is a style of thinking born in Greece and received by Europe as its heritage. The most important "dialogue concerning civilizations" needs to be conducted even more effectively in that same Europe.

---

[46] "Trinidad and Tobago" is the name of an island nation off the coast of Venezuela.

§

In understanding this point, you must consider two elements.

The first is that the concept of an *elite* occupies a deep place in the West. That concept uniquely characterizes the series of religions originating with Judaism. It presupposes a mental and spiritual relationship between those who are "superior" and those who are "inferior." Consequently, real dialogue becomes impossible. For if I am too far superior to you, you just need to listen to me, since you have nothing to offer! The standpoint of Islam is fundamentally the same on this point as that of Judaism and Christianity. Once Levi-Strauss wrote in *Triste tropique*, "Islam is an Occident within the Orient." And this is becoming more and more credible as endorsed by Naipaul. In Christianity and Islam there are common characteristics says Levi-Strauss. They are "evangelizing," "dominating," and "destroying."

If spiritual elitism is the first obstacle to a genuine dialogue of civilizations, a linguistic inferiority complex is the second.

This second point is that from the time of colonialism to the present day, people have made a very strange assumption as they've tried to consider what they call "dialogue." It is assumed that it must be done in a Western language such as English or French. The assumption is made naturally, without reflection. This is not in the consciousness of all those who speak these languages as mother tongue but it is in the minds of Asians and Africans. Even in Japan, there are many who are convinced a priori, when they meet a foreigner, that they must speak in English.

Language is not simply a tool for the transmission of communication. In truth, it transmits culture, and, as I've confidently written already, a language can incarnate a value system. The struggle for hegemony in language is not just an issue of convenience but a battle for hegemony over profound cultural values.

Recently I was requested to do a radio broadcast on French culture, and I was interviewed on the diffusion of the French language in Asia. This seemed to me to be similar to the seminars of bygone days convened to defend French culture (especially against the Anglo-Saxon offensive). I felt the real topic was "Recovery of Share" in the rivalry with English, as being of keen and primary concern to the French people.

The problem is not limited to English and French. Nor is it limited to what languages to designate as official at international conferences, though that is a contentious issue. The fundamental problem is lack of respect for another's language and culture, especially if one party has power and influence superior to the other. Lack of respect and the drive to dominate constitute what we have earlier spoken of as the "subjugation of the spirit." This invisible warfare is not an actual bloody war or the threat of one, but it is the most severe form of war for it concerns the spirit of people. However, it seems to me that modern people tend to be indifferent to anything they cannot see.

When we summarize the two elements mentioned before as having been occasioned by the colonial period, namely, elitism and linguistic hegemony, we can better understand the attitude adopted by Europeans (or by elitist countries with the chosen people idea) who hail their language as the best. They are simply taking an evangelistic attitude toward their language in wishing to impose it on those not fortunate enough to learn it as native speakers. Such an attitude obstructs real dialogue among civilizations. By paying careful attention, we may see in the shadows an effort to substitute one characteristic of Western religions for Western culture. To substitute the *absoluteness* of the revelation of truth for the necessity of continual growth and *improvement* in culture will always produce tragedy. The cultures based on any given religion should not take on the absoluteness of revealed truth as their distinctive posture. For culture is not something that should try to return to, or remain in, static perfection like an eternal God. Culture, as a proper human tool, grows and improves. In fact, it grows by dialogue, by exchange, and by give and take among diverse partners in conversation. If culture adopts the evangelizing or aggressively exclusivistic posture, we must doubt that it can really provide any benefit for the people who practice it.

§

Friend, I would like to consider here the basic form of "information flow." From my point of view, it has two styles. The first style is one by which someone communicates truth to others as revelation; it is a *freely given* act of love typified by Christ. The second is the style by which one *pays for* what one considers to be knowledge of something useful. The prototype of this style is first seen in the give and take of

Socrates and the school of Sophists. In the first style, the flow of information is one-sided. In the second, dialogue becomes possible.[47]

If we call the Christ-model Type One, it is above all else a religious and missionary model for the transmission of information. In contrast to that, Type Two, the Socratic model, must be said to be an educational and scientific kind of communication. This can be adapted to whatever is the current economic sphere. The important thing that here becomes manifest is the problem of the "value" of information. In ancient Athens there were already individuals who judged that knowledge had a value for which money could be paid. In other words, there was already a basic recognition that information is something *profitable for its recipients.* And this is applicable to today's communication technology, economic development, and cultural advancement.

There is an irony here. The West has been proud of the prosperity it gained in the relatively short time of 400 years. Having substituted culture for religion and science for revelation, it remains enthralled by dreams of itself as a Chosen People. Yet its prosperity is due in large part to the sudden rise in power of natural science. The foreign policies of the West now appear to be a double-edged sword hanging over it.

There are missionaries who are not ethnocentric; they share the life of the people where they live, and preach the Gospel assiduously in the local languages. But some state-related agencies imitate the worst examples of missionary activity of the past. These secular missionaries have such names as British Council or *Alliance Française* or American Center. Their chief problem is they confuse culture with God. But for one hundred years, the Japanese have regarded these institutions as Type 2 and so have been willing to pay tuition for information. In the manner of the information-oriented Sophists, these secular institutions have provided instruction in Western languages and cultural matters. But their pedagogy has exemplified Type 1. When they speak like

---

[47] It is common supposition that the Sophists were the first paid teachers in the West but also that Socrates did not accept pay for his interaction with his listeners. Whether the relatively poor Socrates ever received gifts from his better-off students is not the author's point here. The Socratic method was worthy of payment. That method eventuated in the invention of logic and, ultimately, of computer science. Even more important for education and science, the method gave permission for mutuality in dialogue and not just authoritarian monologue.

envoys of Christ, these Western teachers have shown conviction in using authoritarian one-way communication. So there was a gap of understanding between Western teachers and Japanese students about the nature of education in these missionary-like institutions.

§

Let us now return to the matter of language. There is no need for the sweeping lament heard in Japan that Japanese is not an international language. Rather I think Japanese reluctance to insist that their language be used in all international dialogue has played a part in Japanese technological advances until recently vis-à-vis Europe and America. While information from Europe and America flowed in easily, by contrast the flow from Japan to the West was difficult. For the Japanese, the Europeans and Americans have been visible, while for the Westerners, the Japanese have not been visible. While many Japanese did read Western languages, only a small percentage of Westerners read Japanese. It was the Japanese who realized that the transistor theory published by American scientists might be made into a radio. Sony thus became a worldwide company. We may notice that it was after the publication of the American book *Japan As Number One* that the Japanese believed there was nothing to learn anymore and so around 1990 came the crash of the Bubble Economy. For two centuries the West adopted the attitude of those missionaries who emphasized conveying information or dogma to others. Europeans and Americans neglected the importance of learning non-Western cultures and languages. Fundamentalism in any culture prevents learning, while learning from others is essential for the culture itself.

I think the time now approaches when all nations should make themselves available for the dialogue of civilizations. To accomplish that, all human beings must come to recognize the necessity of exerting themselves in the "logic of dialogue."

Letter 10

An Evening with Jacques Cousteau
(1910—1997)

Dear Friend,

My mind goes back to a certain evening when I had a conversation with Jacques Cousteau. Somewhere in my brain arose an image of a tree leaf forming itself into a wonderful fractal pattern, a pattern that shows the exquisite order of the natural realm. That was at the end of 1992. This protector of the global environment, who had been invited to give the keynote address for a world conference of science journalists opening in Tokyo, had on that evening arrived from Paris and invited me for supper at the Imperial Hotel where he was lodged. No sooner had he sat down than Captain Cousteau abruptly broached the subject he wanted to discuss.

C: In my speech tomorrow there will be a philosophical part that may be of special interest to you. Please tell me what you think. It concerns something about the problem of humanity and the law of nature which Hamburger—yes, Jean Hamburger, chair of the French Academy of Science—explained to me three months before he died . . . . As a matter of fact, how many years has it been since *life* manifested itself on earth, or single-cell organisms were born in water?

H: It must have been between three and three and a half billion years ago.

C: How about Homo Sapiens? When did the ancestor of man, appear?

H: Recent discoveries of early humanoids enable us to trace back three or four million years.

C: So, even including Australopithecus, or ape-man as you Japanese say, human life spans a period one-thousandth as long as more ancient forms of life. If we measure from the time of Homo

Sapiens, the time span is only one-ten-thousandth.   As stated in Desmond Morris' metaphor, early man was "the naked ape." It was the fate of human beings originally to be the prey of other species, since humans lacked weapons of offense and defense; that is, they lacked fangs and claws as well as hard protective shells.   However, they conquered the earth. Why do you think that happened?

H: Standing on their two legs freely, they came to use their hands and to discover tools, fire, and so on . . . .

C: Exactly, but there are even more important facts. All life was lived within the "laws of nature." The laws of nature are the laws of the jungle. That is a world of merciless struggle. It's a case of eat or be eaten. Human beings escaped from this law some time in the past and created *their own laws*. Such laws constituted the moral law. Because of the disorders and injustices of the natural phenomena of disease, premature death, and things like that, the notion of *mutual aid* arose. By creating this social order, humanity separated itself from nature, and it is of this "act of divorce" that Hamburger spoke. "Fairness" is not in the language of nature.   Nature exemplifies the rule of unequal opportunity. Within nature, human beings began to create a special space based on a new kind of law introducing the idea of fairness or justice.

H: We have the remains of the Neanderthal old man with the missing hand, don't we? Those remains surely go back 60,000 years. He probably was the keeper of the cave, and it is obvious his family did not abandon him but gave him a role to play. We recognize their feelings of mourning from the flower pollen found with the skeleton.

C: So, we can trace things back to very ancient times. I think we will not be mistaken if we say that moral contracts among human beings were clearly emerging 10,000 years ago.

H: But why did such a thing occur?

C: Well, that is a problem. Why do you think?

H: Wasn't it that they had an encounter with God? [I saw Mr. Cousteau's face turn crimson, and his eyes were shining with excitement.]

C: Precisely. You are right. At that time humans encountered God!

H: That, I think, we may call the discovery of *Logos,*[48] because in the Bible (John 1) is the statement, "In the beginning was the Word."[49] The Word is with God. And the Word becomes God.

C: I think that is correct. Man by means of reason and reasonable expression resisted certain fundamental biological laws. I think that this resistance became the destiny of humankind and gave sense to human life. The opposition to nature's rule, which human reason created, assigned to each individual the new duties of equality, benevolence, and justice. It meant the rejection of the law of the jungle that the strong should eat the weak. And, indeed, it also meant that humanity must rapidly become sovereign in the realm of living things. By shaping their own destiny in such a way, human beings had already made the return to nature impossible. But this same moral contract that brought forth high-level societies, societies that do not exist in other species, is the ironic and fundamental cause of the population explosion and the destruction of the environment that is the main topic of my lecture tomorrow.

H: I am thinking that especially since the 17th century, the assumptions of rationalism and the mechanistic view of nature have created the two-edged sword of progress and destruction. Perhaps all those who have ever shown deep respect or reverence for nature have been simply dismissed as heathen—or else as naive. (Did not Descartes or some of his less restrained followers teach us that nature is merely a non-thinking machine?)

C: It's been 200 years since a declaration of human rights was written, but there are few who understand that human rights are not rights guaranteed by nature. That declaration of human rights was a challenge to the law of nature nurtured by three billion years of life on earth.

H: It's persuasive when we hear such things from a Frenchman.

C: I'd like to tell you a most interesting problem spoken of by Hamburger. The law of the jungle rejected by reason is, nevertheless, carried over in human DNA. That is to say that the whole three-billion-year history of life is imprinted in the human gene. Therefore, in each

---

[48] Or in Japanese, *risei*, which may be translated reason or reasoning power.

[49] The Japanese word this time is *kotoba* (word). "Word" is the more traditional translation of *logos,* but it means both reason and word. In the Bible it even suggests "God in action."

of us there is discord between rational morality and the law of the jungle. The two laws are in a constant state of confrontation.

H: That's a terrific idea. In plain language we have to speak of a rivalry between reason and instinct. However, the point that he advanced referring to the memory of the gene is wonderful. The rational actions of humanity are spoken of as depending on the new cortex of the brain, especially the frontal lobe, but in the old cortex the whole human past is preserved and sometimes sadly manifests itself. Jung seriously considered the unconscious. Moreover, I remember that he was looking for integral man in the interaction between the unconscious and the conscious. It's the "hidden memory" of the human past becoming a collective unconscious, isn't it?

C: I am not one who defends socialism, but I think that in socialism there was fundamentally a point that we have a duty to control that hidden struggle of the mind by reason. However, due to the collapse of the former Soviet bloc, the free market principle is gradually being introduced in socialist countries throughout the world. As a reaction in those countries, the heretofore-repressed law of the jungle now gushes forth all at once. They only demand the free market because of its efficiency . . . . However, no one is asking, "Efficiency for the sake of what?"

Jacques Cousteau, as if he forgot his jet lag, became flushed with excitement. The conversation of just the two of us continued until late that night.

§

Because of the impact of this evening conversation, I could not go to sleep. How startling are such viewpoints! They included an equation and several brief descriptive phrases: encounter of humanity with God = *Logos* and meeting; the establishment of laws exclusively for human beings; the divorce of humanity from nature; the conquest of the earth by man; the destruction of nature; the law of the jungle imprinted in DNA; the conflict of two laws within every human individual . . . . Because of the preeminence of these theories, one could easily think there was no room left for the refutation of any of them.

However, that night in the midst of thoughts and speculations on this and that, I happened to notice something: *In the Orient the "law of nature" is taken to conform to just the "mind of God," isn't it? Nevertheless, if I go along with today's conversation, whatever rejects a natural law becomes God, or is God in the West. Why has such a fundamental difference turned up? Isn't there a hole in this seemingly airtight position? What can that be?* The answer to that flashed into my mind in an instant: Think! *The major premise for that position is in error. The formula—"law of nature" = "law of the jungle" = "eat or be eaten"—is presupposed as granted. However, does the law "eat or be eaten" constitute the law of the jungle? It does not!*

Friend, when I noticed this, I felt within myself a resolving of everything. It felt like the beginning of a rapid unraveling of a tightly wound ball of thread.

The law of the jungle or of Mother Nature is by no means the law of "eat or be eaten." The eaters and the eaten have already been determined. The lion eats the zebra, but the zebra does not eat the lion. The snake eats the frog, but the frog does not eat the snake. Predators and prey are fixed. In this way, everything in nature extending from trees and plants to wild animals circulates fittingly in the ecosystem. The scene in which certain animals become food is brutal and shocking, but even that scene is a link in the maintenance of a species. When there is too great an increase in the numbers of such a species, the increase causes a dwindling in the quantity of plants and, by the same token, a threat to the existence of the species itself. Gnu that have formed a large herd on the African savanna and are in the process of migrating will begin to cross a river in any way necessary. The weak ones that cannot climb up the opposite bank will drown, but I consider this is a kind of "thinning out."

The saying of ancient peoples, "When you want to catch a fish, plant a tree," has been elucidated by recent ecosystem research. Aquatic microorganisms, seaweed, fish, land vegetation, insects, vertebrates—all these occur, recur, and circulate in overall harmony within one great system. Therefore surely that system may be spoken of as due to the providence of God.

People of the Orient, like people of the Occident, witnessed animals killing other animals from ancient times. And haven't they seen deep within this phenomenon what makes it providential? It is the providence of Mother Nature. . . . They, therefore, called this law of nature, God.

Friend, at this time I felt the philosophical profundity of the Orient as perceived in the modern period. This profundity has emerged in some contrast to occidental thinking on nature. If a law of "eat or be eaten" is operative, it is not the law of the jungle. Is it not, instead, a human law? "Wanton violence" is the expression used by the Mexican anthropologist Santiago Genoves as he straightforwardly asserts, "The lion does not murder, the lion only eats." According to him, wanton violence is unique to the human race. It means, in the first place, violence that is not directly for food, and, secondly, killing for reasons other than the continued existence of one's own species. This is something not seen in other animal species. (Exceptionally, gorillas that are primates and closely related to human beings have reportedly been seen killing other gorillas.) Genoves supposes that outbreaks of such violence towards each other arose with the first human revolution, that is, the beginning of agriculture.   And certainly since then, humanity has composed a bloody history of killing or being killed.

§

The 17th-century English philosopher Thomas Hobbes spoke of humans as a wolf species, Homo Homini Lupus. He means that human beings act predatory toward each other. He concludes in his classic book, *Leviathan*, that human beings should abandon private rights and should give them to the sovereign or the state in exchange for the maintenance of order. Long ago this became the basis for socialism.

In the Orient, three centuries before the Christian era, the great scholar Xun-zi (Hsün Tzu) set forth the doctrine that human nature is evil. This was during the last part of the Warring States period in China. "Man by nature is evil; virtue must be cultivated," Xun-zi teaches. In other words, the true character of human beings is selfish, so virtue is something that is created by effort in a proper moral and educational environment. This is the philosophy of a turbulent age. Confucianists had placed authority and power in Heaven, but Xun-zi, with his realistic view of the world's turbulence, denied Heaven. He separated Heaven and humanity and denied that either human rights or metaphysical value should be based on Heaven. Instead of asceticism he advocated fulfilling human desires moderated by propriety. This way of thinking of moderation is intelligible in terms of what Aristotle the Greek, at nearly the same time, called "the golden mean."

The teachings of Jesus Christ, when carefully looked at, constitute a doctrine based on the evil nature of humanity, the need for repentance and for passage through a "narrow gate" into the Kingdom of God whose great love, coupled with a sincere quest for conversion, promises salvation to the faithful. This love of God preached by Jesus is, however, presented to everyone, and is close to the Buddha's Great Mercy and Great Compassion.

My aim now is not to go deeply into these doctrines, but what I would like to say here is that before and during the Middle Ages, regardless of whether one lived in the East or the West, all of the excellent authoritative teachings raised the question of Value as they spoke of how people should live. In this long period, even science did not separate itself from questions of value.

However, what we have called modern science since the 17th century separates itself, by and large, from philosophy and ethics. The tendency to sever subject from object and to look at everything objectively is exactly like what journalists began to create with their "zero-degree" style that had no room for any personal thinking or feeling. Such a style sets up a "value free" or even "valueless" principle. This is what justified for the first time the position that the divine life is not seen within nature. That position divides all entities into two kinds and so creates the dualism of subject and object. The "scientific" attitude severs nature as object from the conscious subject observing it. This attitude is based on the twofold idea that (1) the reason resident in the human brain is infinitely close to God, and (2) that what is opposed to it, namely, nature including "the body," is exclusively physical, hence governed by the principle of struggle called the law of the jungle or by the oriental word "karma." Descartes, whom I am primarily critiquing here, saw nature as perfect but like a perfect watch. It becomes only a machine. What I am criticizing is his radical dualism of subject and object that devitalizes nature. In the *Summa Theologica* by the greatest medieval theologian, Thomas Aquinas, is the description of nature's deficiency or privation, "*Natura est privatio.*" This is what I think directly presages the position of Descartes.

The Scholastics of the Sorbonne in the 13thcentury constructed a grand plan to fuse Christian theology and Greek rationalism, particularly with the philosophy of Aristotle. Ironically, this synthesis paved the way for the rejection of their ideology. This work eventually led to the scientism that skeletonized Christianity. However, Aristotle himself in his essay on the soul (*De Anima*) argued that the highest level, which is the human soul, includes in itself the vegetative and animal souls from the lower levels.

Recent psychologists, especially those of the Jungian school, point out that the mind is not limited to consciousness but includes the unconscious and the body as well. From that point of view, such importance was at one time attributed to matter as to raise it to divine status. Included among those who think like this are the medieval alchemists who sought for the integrity or wholeness of human nature which contains both mind and body. Furthermore, exponents of the Jungian school find in the mandala, which is an integrated perception of the universe, the most adequate symbol for the wholeness of human life. Support for such wholeness has come out also in the recent UNESCO sponsored seminar on "Culture and Science." It involves the inseparability of body and mind, and of subject and object.[50] I consider that the meaning of existence reveals itself right in the middle of this *wholeness* or "complete oneness" of existence. In the coming century, the problem of *value* must be considered from this point of view.

§

Friend, let us look at the thought patterns of some of the world's aborigines. In Peru, where the Amazon River issues from the Andes Mountains, members of the Machigenga tribe who live in the Manu National Park talk to plants and use herbs for medicine. They are convinced that everything has a soul. For the Inuit of Canada, "spirits of the woods" exist. The thinking of the Ainu in Japan is similar.

When I see the modern world rushing forward centered solely on the human function of reason, I think that the time has come for reason itself to ask reconsideration of its supremacy. The primitive wisdom called shamanism or animism that was once looked down on has become a stimulus for such reconsideration. We can say that this reconsideration is a movement to reinstate the *sensitivity* lost by modern rationalism.

---

[50] The Zen expression for this is *shukyaku mibun*. The unity of the individual human life is the point here, just as unity of the (reinterpreted) law of the jungle with the overarching Providence of God was the point earlier in the present chapter. The author's underlying conviction is that Providence works through nature indirectly and through human life directly to preserve and enhance Value. This approach, above all, is intended to present a viable alternative to the kind of extreme dualism associated historically with Zoroastrianism.

Jacques Cousteau had a wonderful experience at the environmental conference in Rio de Janeiro. He'd been invited to a gathering of minority peoples that was occurring at the same time as the meeting of governments. Representatives of the minority peoples were hoisting a flag to show their solidarity. At just the moment when the flag reached the top of its pole in the outdoor meeting place, an eagle from out of nowhere perched on top of the pole.

Cousteau concluded his lecture in Tokyo with a citation from Gregory Bateson: "It is equally monstrous and dangerous to separate intellect from emotion . . . as to separate mind from body."

Michelangelo's Pieta, Museum of the Opera del Duomo in Florence

Crest of arms on façade of Santa Trinita Church

Letter 11

The Image of God

Dear Friend,

The unfinished Pieta, one of the last datable works of Michelangelo, is located in the quiet, nearly deserted museum of the Cathedral of Florence. I was captured by a strange and deep feeling as I stood in front of this major work in marble that the 80-year-old Renaissance master is thought to have left, according to someone's opinion, as the tombstone for himself.

Surrounding Christ who has been taken down from the cross are, on the right, Mary his mother, holding fast her own son who has been put to death, and, on the left, under his right arm, Mary Magdalene. But also behind Jesus in this Pieta there is a huge person. This man, who is covered up to his face by his outer garment, is not yet identified with certainty. However, at that time I felt, "This is God." I have no explanation for the feeling. It was just the way I felt. My daughter Cordelia, who was a student at the University of Fine Arts of the Louvre, sensed my feeling and said, "Don't think a stupid thing like that! It is said that this figure represents Philip, who was present when Jesus was taken down from the cross." But for me, my intuition at that time was more important than an academic theory.

And my intuition changed into conviction on the next day. Guided by Fabricio Lelli, a young historian living in Florence, we visited the Church of Santa Trinita (the Holy Trinity). That church attracts few tourists. In a coat of arms displayed on the facade of the church there clearly appears a Pieta made in the same Renaissance era. In the background just above Jesus, who has been taken down from the cross, stands God the Father; on the right, sits the holy mother; and, on the left, kneels Magdalene. The arrangement of these figures is identical with that of the other Florentine Pieta with the exception of the dove representing the Holy Spirit.

Just then a thought began to run around in my head. I said to myself, "Sometime during the Renaissance, the image of God was created. And wouldn't Michelangelo, knowing he was near the end of his life, wish to carve an image of God that would be uniquely relevant to his own life as a man? It was as though God were a father watching over and protecting him personally . . . ."

The Most Holy Being cannot be pictured or sculpted. Shinto in Japan felt the same way. Portraits of the emperors who were regarded as divine are presented much less often than portraits of the shoguns. And it will come as no surprise to Western readers that the Creator is never represented artistically in Judaism or Christianity. In the Old Testament world, and to a lesser extent in the New Testament, manifestations of God take the form of light or voice. In Islam, with its strict monotheism, God is conceived as a unique and absolute being that must not be duplicated in art, nature, or humanity. For all three religions, then, it was unthinkable to make figures of the Creator.

However, the Renaissance was a period that embraced *the revival of the human and of the beauty of form.* As a small fraction of painters were tempted by the humanized form of the gods of Mt. Olympus in ancient Greece, they timidly left us canvases and frescoes containing the prohibited representations of God the Father. But, as we witness in the paintings of Michelangelo in the Sistine Chapel in Rome, God is portrayed only as he appears in Genesis. Although passages in Genesis concerning the creation were by now generally accepted in a more mythological sense, Michelangelo even dared represent God as an old man creating Adam. And other paintings of this same period portrayed God creating animals and fish. And yet when the period passed, this trend in painting disappeared. And, as far as I know, in the field of sculpture there is not a single other example. Apart from the Renaissance, there are no other artistic images of God the Father as Creator.

On the other hand, statues and images of Jesus and of Mary came to be created in great numbers with the rise of the Medieval adoration of the Holy Mother. Among those, we see the example of Chartres where the goddesses of the native faith of Druidism are transformed into the Black Mary venerated now in the Christian context. The themes most often dealt with include the sufferings (Passion) of Jesus, along with Mary holding the infant Jesus.

§

My friend, an image of the hill of Golgotha comes to my mind. The mother hiding herself in the crowd sees her own son being nailed to the cross. Then from the mouth of that dying man she hears uttered a fearful word spoken in a surprisingly loud voice to those in the vicinity: "*Eli, Eli, lama sabachthani,*" that is, "My God, my God, why have you forsaken me?" Isn't this a word that freezes the blood of all true Christians? At the time of Jesus' death there is the awful doubt that God the Father does not watch over his own Son; or perhaps the Father God does not exist. Doesn't this involve the very depth of despair? The disciples disappeared after having received Christ's flesh and blood with the evening meal on the previous day. At the side of Jesus when he was lowered from the cross is the mother who had to witness the execution of her own son. On the other side, there is Mary Magdalene the woman who most loved Jesus.

However, God the Father *was* watching over his Son. The resurrection of Christ on the third day, as prophesied, is evidence for this and a vindication of this presence. Friend, the *resurrection* of Christ is, indeed, the core of Christianity. Because of that, the Father must be present at that very moment.

When we see it like this, for the first time we understand the meaning of Michelangelo's Florentine Pieta. At the time of the death of his son who died shouldering the sin of humankind, the Father appears showing his own compassion through the look of great love with which he embraces his son. The Father is greater than the son. And the mother is greater than Mary Magdalene. Here, in Michelangelo's work, is preserved the special measure of a quite universal religious artistry.

What I perceive the 80-year-old master sought to sculpt into this Pieta was *resurrection,* not death, and *hope,* not despair. Isn't it possibly true that this Pieta carved by Michelangelo might have become his own tombstone? Now I understand how that other wonderful Pieta, the one in Milan that shows Christ rising after the crucifixion to bear his mother on his shoulders, has the same meaning as the Florentine sculpture though the image is radically changed. Both works are signs of resurrection.

Friend, standing before this Pieta in Florence, I hurried my thoughts back in time to ancient Hellenism. Greek civilization that had made a *declaration of humanity* went on to encounter one after another various

cultures strange to it. The period was one of *dialogue among cultures.*
Hellenism, proceeding east by the roads trodden by Alexander the
Great, had encountered Buddhism in the land of Gandhara[51] in the first
century A.D., about the time of the Kushan Dynasty[52]. If this contact
with Hellenism had not happened, would Buddha ever have been
represented as a human figure? After the death of Buddha 500 years
earlier, his personality was considered too sacred to be transformed into
human form and so was represented only by symbols such as the holy
tree of enlightenment (the Bodhi tree), the stupa, a footprint, or the
wheel of law (chakra). When artists finally presented the human figure
of the Buddha, that fact gave keen assistance to Buddhist growth and
influence. Why? Because human beings by their very nature seek
form.

In the upper Indus valley there are images of Buddha carved into the
rock. These were probably made by the Gandhara people driven into
the mountains by fear of persecution from the non-Buddhists. What
gave them the will to survive in the severely cold Karakoram
mountains? Wasn't it the human form of the Buddha that they carried
in their hearts and carved into the mountain sides?

---

[51] *Gandhara* (also *Gandhāra*)—an ancient region in what is presently northwest
Pakistan, constituted in part by the Vale of Peshāwar, and a meeting place
between India, Central Asia, and the Middle East.   See Britannica's
Micropaedia for details.

[52] *Kushan Dynasty.* This dynasty "descended from the Yuëh-Chih, a people
that ruled over most of the northern Indian subcontinent, Afghanistan, and parts
of Central Asia during the first three centuries of the Christian era." They
spread Buddhism in Central Asia and China and developed Mahayana
Buddhism and the Gandhara school of art. *Micropaedia,* Vol. 7, p. 46.

© 2000 LAEL PORTER

The triangle formed by the three cities of Swat, Peshāwar, and Taxila indicates the ancient region of Gandhara. Taxila was its capital and is a jewel of modern archeology. Swat was the birthplace of both Mahayana Buddhism and the Bodisattvas as important components of Buddhist philosophy and religion. And Peshāwar is said to have been important as a terminus for caravans from Afghanistan as well as a center for culture; it is located nine miles from the southern entrance to the Khyber Pass. In the modern city is found the Peshāwar Museum containing notable sculptures from the Gandhara civilization.

Letter 12

The Birth of Perspective

Dear Friend,

Several years ago when I was in the Kremlin Palace in Moscow, I went to a chapel that has the onion-shaped domes characteristic of czarist Russia. The icons filling the walls emerged from the dark in golden color and gave rise to a strange solemnity.

At that time the Russian archeologist accompanying me said something interesting. According to him, the drawing of an icon is like the creation story found in Genesis. There is a board with nothing but chaos on it. Then God says, "Let there be light." Therefore, over the whole surface of the board, gold is painted. The forms are going to be drawn on the gold; the human face will be painted last. This sequence of painting follows the order of creation in Genesis.

Over time the religious paintings that have preserved the Byzantine tradition got blackened with soot from the candles that lit the churches. Many of the icons are repainted ones. Because several layers of paint were eventually applied to the same side of the boards, they naturally became warped. Each painting that overlaid previous works utilized the same order of production used through the centuries.

I learned from the Russian scholar that icons are manifestations of God's world itself. Byzantine art does not represent scenery as seen by man. There is no human viewpoint. Even *time* does not exist. I reached the conclusion that all these are very human things—the passing of time, the appearance of movement, and the three-dimensional world.

§

The technique of perspective in paintings was born in the Renaissance period. However, it is not just a technique of drawing three dimensions in two; it also signifies a fundamental transformation of our view of humanity. Even if the religious scene pictured is the same as in the past, the nature of the painting is completely different. Now the subjective existence of man outside of the painted scene is taken into consideration. In the icon, man is just a part of the world of God, but now man is on the outside looking in. It seems to me that this matter is deeply involved with the "rediscovery of humanity" in the Renaissance.

Moreover, the Renaissance does more than just revive the Greek view, since it moves toward the establishment of the individual *self.* This is in fact the fulfillment of Greek rationalism. Reason is fundamentally the function that divides one thing from another. It even distinguishes good from evil, but, above all, it distinguishes subject from object. The self which became subject sees an object—a religious scene, nature, or a street in a town. This is the structure that gave birth to the perspective method. Everything is *objectified.* This is not what happens in the world of the icon, because there the icon itself is the *reality.*

When we say "perspective" we often think of painting, but it applies to other examples, such as Le Nôtre's city planning in the 17th century. He drew the straight lines of the Champs-Élysées away from the Tuileries Palace, and also those of the Grand Canal, as viewed from the Hall of Mirrors in Versailles. The point is this: what a painting has in common with a geometrical garden is that *a single visual point of view is established.*

One's glance has to start from this unique viewing point. The viewer could be a king or any one else. If the viewing point is plural, the three-dimensional world of perspective will never appear. The parallel lines of a road in perspective converge at the top of the triangle. If no single viewpoint is chosen, the convergence cannot happen. Nor could an object have a shadow without perspective.

Friend, when I was in the Academia Museum of Venice, I observed the shift toward the individual human viewpoint and away from the omnipresent glance of God. We can clearly see this shift in this museum's collection. In Venice, which was closely tied to Eastern cities such as Constantinople, a Byzantine ambiance permeates every nook and cranny of the city.   St. Mark's Cathedral is an eminent example of this.

In the first room of the Academia Museum, you can see the works of early artists.   The Byzantine influence in the 14th and 15th century altar paintings extend from Paulo Veneziano to Michele Giambono.   As you move to the next room, you note the beginnings of depicting things at a distance, and, along with that, the shift toward the use of perspective as exemplified by Piero della Francesca (1420—1492)[53]. The Renaissance painter, Giovanni Bellini (1430—1516)[54], has already made the transition.   His figures of the Holy Mother and Christ are realistically human.   Landscape painting was born in this way and was developed by later masters of the Venetian school, such as Gentile Bellini and Vittore Carpaccio, when they painted events that occurred on the streets of Venice.

Now we go to Florence where Michelangelo established a single viewpoint in sculpture.   Before Michelangelo began to cut anything from the Carrara marble, he sketched the front view of the sculpture on the most beautiful side of the block of marble.   His technique from that point is known as Michelangelo's direct carving which means that he first chisels a relief along the lines of his sketch, then a high relief, and finally on the other side of the marble, he proceeds in the same way. The important thing is the existence of this single viewpoint that explains the fact that if he stopped work anywhere in the process of production, there was already a work of art.   And some of his pieces did stop before a fully three-dimensional figure could emerge.

We must pay attention here to the fact that the birth of perspective implies not only the human viewpoint but the establishment of the human as an individual.   It was not an affirmation of humanity as a mass.   Even when a crowd is looking at something, the object is not seen by all eyes but only by one pair.

As we take note of these things, we can understand why the art of perspective did not exist in many Asian countries including Japan.   The

---

[53] Piero della Francesca, according to Encarta 98, was an "Italian painter of the first rank, whose style was one of the most individual of the early Renaissance."

[54] Bellini was the "presiding genius of early Renaissance painting in Venice, and an artist of world rank." *Microsoft Encarta 98 Encyclopedia,* 1993—1997 Microsoft Corporation. All rights reserved.

picture scroll of *The Tale of Genji* simply tells the sparkling tale itself.
It contains no individual *viewpoint of an outside person.* If that were
the case, it would be as though a god is gazing on the characters from a
cloud above roofless houses where the characters are unaware that their
roofs have disappeared. In contrast, consciousness of each character
flows from right to left in the scroll. Similarly, in the Islamic sphere of
South Asia, pictures came to have more and more ornamental designs.
Lacking a single viewpoint, they became an art form in which objects
cannot even cast a shadow.

Perhaps it's possible that certain Chinese paintings were close to the
perspective method. These emerged in the southern school of Chinese
mountain hermits. Their Zen ink drawings depicted light and shadow
which evoke the profundity of nature. At that point artists as *isolated
individuals* disappear because of a oneness with nature.[55] This kind of
art is going to attract people who see into mysterious depths. In a
living scene, the lines of geometry used to show perspective do not
appear. So "powerful glances" that dissolve everything and every
person into the perspective of an object are antithetical to the spirit of
Zen. Delacroix uses the powerful gaze of a unique human viewer in
his battle scenes of Napoleon. In the same way, the painter David
shows us a single human view in his Sabine women; we see the story
unfolding as if on a stage before a spectator. Such an arrangement is
not seen in the Japanese scroll of a battle.

§

Friend, the scholasticism that reached its peak in the 13th century
was a grand attempt to mix Hellenic rationalism with Hebraic faith.
What Thomas Aquinas seems to have miraculously done is like mixing
oil and water. With the passage of time a separation will occur just as
when the vinegar in a French salad dressing eventually separates from
the olive oil. The medieval period, then, was a time of unstable
synthesis. The time of its collapse was the Italian Renaissance, which
rediscovered the Hellenic view of human nature and reason. On the
other hand, Martin Luther in Germany preached a return to God that is
known as the Protestant Reformation. This movement represents an
ideology akin in some respects to the various forms of fundamentalism
in today's world. Given enough time, water and oil will separate.

---

[55] The philosophical term for the realization of such a disappearance is *Mu,* or
Nothingness.

The Renaissance began in 15th-century Italy as the restoration of humanism. While the Copernican revolution was occurring, there was a shift from the divine viewpoint to the human, and the Renaissance moved northward to France eventuating in the 16th-century French Renaissance. I consider this intimately relates to Descartes' concept of an absolute and isolated ego in the 17th century.

Once the serpent spoke to the woman in the Garden of Eden, "If you eat this fruit, your eyes will open and you will become as gods knowing good and evil." This means, "You will become equal to God." For once what the serpent said was not a deception. It was the truth. Humans who ate the forbidden fruit have not only become equal to God, they have killed God (in the phraseology of Nietzsche). Isn't that the history of escape from the medieval period? The birth of perspective is the strange and wonderful transformation of the "ones who are seen by God" into "ones who see God."

Part III. Invisible Threads Connecting Civilizations

Letter 13

The Hidden Stream

Dear Friend,

Do you know Bahrain? It's a small island floating in the Persian Gulf. In documents dating from about the time of Alexander the Great, this island was mentioned; for travellers from lands of heat and desert, it was indeed the "pearl of the Persian Gulf." The fact of Bahrain's being considered a land of bliss can even be recognized from its having a vast cluster of ancient tombs covering the central area of the southern part of the island. After carrying their dead there, rich people from Arabia constructed gravesites on sacred ground that was believed to give them ready access to the kingdom of heaven.

From ancient times this island was called Dilmun or Delmon. (Since there is no way of inscribing vowels in the Arabic language, spelling varies depending on the vowel chosen in the Roman alphabet.) The name signifies "two waters" and refers to the fact that fresh water as well as salt water favor the island. As is the case in almost every country of the Near and Middle East, rainfall is limited to only one season. As would be expected, inland Bahrain has a desert look. However, there is an inland place where a clear spring gushes forth.

It is the Spring of Hadali near Manama, the capital and the only large city in the country. This is a sacred spring flowing into a stone-lined pond. The diameter would perhaps be twenty meters (60 feet) and the depth at its deepest place, five meters (15 feet). Wonder of wonders!. We see pure, dark bluish water gushing forth. To find this spring in such a flat and arid land is mysterious enough, but when I gaze into its depths, can I believe my eyes? I see several large fish serenely swimming around—or am I dreaming? At first I wonder whether the fish, which approach 50 cm (20 inches) in length, are carp, but when I look carefully, their shape is different. I seek information from the Bahraini friend accompanying me, but he also does not know the fish's name. We agree that its form resembles the *hamour,* a fish that is relished in Bahrain.

However, the *hamour* is a sea fish. Then how did the fish get here and when? To that question, I got the following answer: "These sacred fish were already here when the spring was discovered long ago. No one fishes in this sacred pool." If that is true, have these fish been living here since the time of Alexander? Does that mean that these fish lived for 2,300 years through long-departed histories with this twenty-meter pond as their only world? A deep and strange feeling seized me as I contemplated this. However, no matter how sacred this fish is, it must have a natural life span. What suddenly caught my eye near the surface of the water was a teeming mass of innumerable three-quarter-inch young fish. Were they possibly the answer? But between the large and the very small ones there were are no middle-sized fish—something contrary to the normal life cycle. The riddle would not go away.

One idea arose during the process of my fantastic cerebrations: *Perhaps these fish know that the amount of water in this pond only allows seven grown fish to live here at one time. Consequently, until the grown fish die it is the destiny of the smaller fish hatched here to die. However, at a certain time, the lives of the present seven grown fish will end. Then selected ones of the young fish will survive, and so in this way, the sacred fish will circulate forever.*

Suddenly there came into my brain the image of a bamboo forest in Sagano, the western region of Kyoto. In a beautiful bamboo grove, once every hundred years the bamboo trees flower; after that all the bamboo withers. However, in the spring of the next year, new bamboo shoots will produce new clumps.

This may be similar to what happened in the 3rd century B.C. when, according to tradition, King Aśoka's daughter carried to Ceylon a branch of the bodhi tree under which Buddha Shākyamuni received enlightenment. That branch became the great tree in the Temple of the Bodhi Tree in the ancient Ceylonese city of Anurādhapura. That tree also is subject to a life cycle. It renews itself through many generations, with shoot after shoot being generated from the original tree.

This Bodhisattva
appears in a mural in
the Buddha Hall of
Horyuji.

On a rock shelf at the
ruins of Sigiriya are
images of heavenly
maidens.

§

Friend, I was in Sri Lanka (Ceylon) several years ago. There is a cultural triangle formed by the three ancient cities of Anurādhapura, Polonnaruwa, and Kandy—cities that were scattered but linked. UNESCO plans to restore and preserve their ruins as a Cultural Legacy of Humankind. In Kandy, a tooth of Buddha is venerated as a relic of great fame. And proceeding north from there, we see a number of ruins that remind us of the images of the ancient dynasties of Ceylon. Dambulla, located almost at the center of this triangle, is a temple complex in the natural rock caverns halfway up a stone mountain. The cavern temples are filled with colorful murals to their very ceilings. Hundreds of impressive Buddhist images painted in strange shades of yellow and a huge nirvanic Buddha were all sealed away for 2,000 years in these temples. Today they have become objects of devotion.

When we go about twelve miles northeast through a forest devoid of inhabited villages, suddenly a mysterious rock mass appears above a sea of foliage. This is Sigiriya. Formed like the 650-foot-high command tower of a submarine, the stony mountain is encircled by steep cliffs. On first appearance it is awe-inspiring and unapproachable. However, Prince Kashapa, who had murdered his royal father in the 5th century B. C., built a palace on the top of this mountain and constructed vast water and rock gardens at its foot.[56] The many holes drilled in rows suggest the existence of dwellings and a water irrigation system created by linking the rocks skillfully together with a brick foundation. And on the rocky cliff facing west and rising vertically for 165 feet from the rock garden, we find wondrous rock drawings inside an overhanging shelter. These paintings include a group of buxom beauties drawn in such a way that we may say the work is still erotic. Twenty-one drawings remain in nearly perfect condition. They probably represent little groups of heavenly maidens because all are drawn as if clouds are hiding their lower parts. They are patterned after high ranking ladies wearing bracelets and necklaces, but the upper half of their bodies are bare showing their naked breasts. Their hair ornaments and crowns tell of their noble rank. In recent years a narrow iron stairway has been installed so the rock shelf can be climbed. In this place, where even a foothold is precarious, who would

---

[56] According to *Micropaedia,* this stronghold was known as Lion Mountain and was built in 477 A.D. "Visitors began the final ascent through the open jaws and throat (*giriya*) of a monumental lion (*sinha*), thus Sigiriya."

have ever wanted to paint these pictures? And for what purpose? That is still a riddle.

But, friend, my attention was attracted to a particular aspect of the painting, that is, the crown that each of the beauties is wearing. I thought that somewhere else I had seen a similar crown with a large jewel inserted in the front. However, what I noticed here was the position of that crown in relation to the face. The beautiful women are drawn very realistically and dynamically, and their faces without exception are each turned to the right or the left. But, in several cases, the crowns they are wearing are facing forward. I thought, "The crowns seem to be slipping."

It is 4 o'clock and the setting sun shines under the rock eaves. As I stand before the heavenly maidens of Sigiriya, who rise in flight bewitchingly, my mind goes back thirty years to the Far East, to the Japan of the Tempyō/Nara period (710—794). *This is the image of the Bodhisattva in the Buddha Hall of Horyuji, isn't it?* I recalled that there at Horyuji was a Bodhisattva image similar to this one; it had been lost in an unfortunate fire and repaired afterwards. That buxom Bodhisattva also had a crown facing the front while her face was turning slightly to the left. It was clear that the crown had been redrawn, because its original lines remain faint in the background. I remember there was some discussion as to whether, because of the repair work, the original lines would ever be restored.

Should we think of this as a coincidence? No, it could never be so. These two pictures of Sigiriya and Nara are drawn according to exactly the same principle. In ancient Egypt they had a different principle: the face turned to one side and the eyes looked to the front. So isn't it possible at a certain time that one style of Buddhist painting was adopted in both Sri Lanka and Horyuji? When the face is turned, the crown showing heavenly-bestowed rank must face the front. This would account for the crown being first drawn facing the same way as the head, then (still in antiquity) being repainted to face forward though the head is still turned, as we see it in the picture.

It would be foolish to suppose the crown's position a mistake. It is unthinkable that artists would mindlessly restore without tracing the original lines even now visible to the eye. Maybe a foreign monk inspired an *intentional* restoration of the painting according to a new principle. The important fact is that in Sri Lanka as well as in Japan, the principle was brought in from the outside. The wall paintings of

Sigiriya, which are unique in Sri Lanka, are linked to Horyuji in Japan by an invisible thread. What is this "outside" and which route made the invisible linkage?

Of course, what I first thought of was India. Certainly the beautiful women of Sigiriya, who are overflowing with carnal shapeliness, are like ones we see in one type of Indian art. When we consider both the area of northern India where the Sinhalese[57] come from and the transmission of Buddhism in the 3rd century B.C. by Prince Mahinda, son of King Aśoka, it is natural to think of India as the "outside" that was closest. There is a legend that the Buddha himself stayed at Kelaniya east of Colombo. However, this nearby India with its beautiful women is not necessarily a friendly neighbor, as successive battles with the Tamils in South India show us. And India returned to Hinduism while Sri Lanka remains a Buddhist country.

§

Friend, I would like here to consider the silk roads or what earlier we have called "the silk roads of the sea." At Polonnaruwa excavations have revealed perfect snow-white porcelain of the Northern and Southern Song[58] dynasties (10th—13th century), but, according to Chinese literature, exchange between China and Sri Lanka traces back to 1 A.D. when Ceylonese royal envoys brought tribute to the Chinese emperor. What's more, for at least five centuries Chinese monks visited Sri Lanka. In Anurādhapura, the capital from the 4th till the 11th century, there were several Hinayana Buddhist monasteries as well as the monastery Abhayagiri (temple of liberation from fear) which became a base of operations for Mahayana Buddhism. The Abhayagiri Monastery had several thousand monks at one time. Many of these Ceylonese monks crossed into China. Which route did they take? They travelled by sea on the route used by the Greeks, Romans, Saracens, Indians, and Chinese—a route linking Alexandria to Canton. It is because of this historical fact that we understand the close relationsɪɪɪp between the royal family of the Sinhalese dynasty and those of Indonesia and Burma.

Doubtless the Abhayagiri Monastery in Ceylon was under the influence of the Chinese Mahayana school and so Chinese Mahayana monks visited there on their pilgrimages. Later the monastery was

---

[57]Sinhalese = Ceylonese

[58] *Song. "Sung"* was an earlier spelling of this Chinese dynastic name.

defeated in a power struggle with the Hinayana branch and finally, by imperial command in the 12th century, it became an abandoned temple. It is clear that the name "China" (Shina) was erased from the literature left there.

China welcomed many Ceylonese monks, especially 8th century China. Ch'ang-an, the Chinese model for Kyoto and Nara in Japan, was a hustling, bustling, crowded international city of Chinese, Indians, Persians, Javanese, Japanese, Koreans and others, so it is not surprising that Japanese student monks met Ceylonese monks there. And in this way Buddhist culture came to Japan. Certain scholars argue for the possibly direct influence of a Ceylonese monk on the establishment of the Shingon sect by Kūkai (774—835). Huidong who transmitted the law (Dharma) to Kūkai received the law from Indian monks named Vajrabodhi and Amoghavajra. What's more, if we consider the Mahā-Vairochana[59] Sutra, it was a monk from a Western country[60] who made a Chinese version of this sutra. So, naturally this possibility of influence from Ceylon comes to mind.

I consider that perhaps in the eighth and ninth centuries, the Mahayana group that built Borobudur in Java had some linkages with the Ceylonese Mahayanist school. If I am right, the affection with which the Japanese regard Borobudur can be understood in terms of the thread of cultural interchange provided by the sea silk route as it linked the Indian Ocean to the seas of South China and East China.

Friend, I feel almost like a 5th-century Chinese monk witnessing the scene of 35 ships anchored and waiting for the trade winds in the Mantai Harbor on the northwest part of Sri Lanka. In my mind's eye I also see the 15th century scene of Zheng He's great fleet of 125 warships and other vessels conquering the seas off the west coast of Sri Lanka. Is the early relationship of the land routes with the sea routes close to the 21st century relationship of sea routes and air routes? In both cases, wonderful cultural exchange is carried out with remarkable

---

[59] According to the article "Vairochana" by Geoffrey Parrinder in his *A Dictionary of Non-Christian Religions* (Philadelphia: The Westminster Press, 1971), "This solar deity perhaps entered Buddhism through the connection between the Buddha and light. . . . In Java Vairochana was regarded as the supreme Buddha, and so he is to the Shingon sect in Japan, where he is represented by a huge statue at Nāra. He is also called Mahā-Vairochana, 'great'."
[60] That means any country west of China.

speed. In future research into the history of East-West interchange, I am convinced that more light should be directed toward things carried by sea. What are now thought to be distinct and separate phenomena will probably then be more clearly understood, and we will notice that invisible and long-forgotten threads of waterways once linked these phenomena. This brings us back to our riddle of Bahrain.

Recently scientists discovered a large underground layer of water beneath the desert of Saudi Arabia. We are almost certain that an underground vein extends to Bahrain from this fresh water storage tank. In the middle of the ocean off the northwest part of this island there is a place where this vein has partially broken and now fresh water gushes forth. This area was known from ancient times both as rich fishing grounds and a place of production for the pearls of Bahrain. The divers for these pearls dive into the sea with leather bags, and they collect not only pearls but also *fresh water.* This collection of fresh water from the sea bottom may perhaps explain what is meant by the expression "two waters."

Here the *hamour's* young fish, conditioned by water that has become less salty, could live in that fresh-water fault. A few might survive to be drawn through the underground vein and to be discharged into the Spring of Hadali. All these things could be considered as possibilities. Of course, this is simply a hypothesis, but the recent discovery of an underground vein of water gives us clarification at least of the source of the Hadali spring.[61]

---

[61] To the question we started with, namely, how did seven full-size fresh water fish happen to turn up in this desert pond and survive here for so many centuries, the main possible answers seem to be the ones indebted to fantasy (1 and 2 below) and the ones indebted to a more scientific approach (3 and 4).

• The fish are immortal, placed here by the gods.
• Because of the limited amount of water, the mature fish "know" that they must sometime make way for the small fish if the sustainable number of seven is to survive. But there are no medium-sized fish.
• The amount of space allows seven and only seven mature fish to survive, but when seven disappear at the same time, then seven of the smaller fish will become the new generation. Here, then, we have the riddle of the Spring of Hadali.
• From time to time adult-sized fish may enter from the underground stream (Hattori doubts this.)

This analysis is the translator's and is in the Western philosophical/scientific tradition of Descartes and other early modern thinkers. Eiji Hattori, as a

Friend, what has not been clear is whether there is some direct relation between Sigiriya as a set of non-religious ruins, and Anurādhapura as a temple metropolis similar to Nara and Kyoto. Nevertheless, when I visited a monastery called "the Western monastery" in the suburb or Anurādhapura, I became convinced of the existence of this relationship.

A different perspective on this monastery comes from Roland Silva, the head of the Cultural Bureau of Sri Lanka. He says it was a meditation monastery (neither Mahayana nor Theravada) where the monks rejected Buddha images, avoided decorations, and were living the simple life in a group. Was the rule of this monastery similar to Zen practice? The answer to this question became more clear as I stood amidst these ruins. They constitute a structure surrounded by water. If one were to replace the water with sand, it would become a rock garden exactly like Ryoanji in Kyoto (called a Zen garden by Westerners). In this way, the threads connecting Sigiriya and Nara gradually revealed themselves to me. I remember also that the rock fountains in the village of Asuka near Nara share the same techniques with the lotus-shaped fountain in Sigiriya.

There seem to be comparable resemblances between the dolmens found in Karnak, in South Bretagne (Brittany) or Stonehenge in England, and in the "Stone Stage" at Asuka village. Is there a good way to make the invisible threads more visible? I am thinking of the crow-goblin masks (so like *tengu* in Japan) which nurture the Canadian Indians called "Cedar People." The migrations of groups of Asians across the Bering Straits (according to the well-accepted theory) keep these similarities from being only accidental agreements of cultures at great distances from each other.

---

modern Japanese author, uses this approach but also starts from a subtly but importantly different point: mystery and wonder rather than exclusively the formation, testing, and revision or rejection of each hypothesis. Perhaps because the hypotheses are inconclusive, his more Japanese approach allows us to share his wonder at the original discovery of the spring-fed pond or his sense of the suggestive possibility that threads of underground linkage provide a significant metaphor for the silk roads at the ground's surface. The very incompleteness of Hattori's discussion reminds us of a Zen black and white painting, suggestive of more than it tells. Perhaps the best solution to the riddle of the fish is to admit that there is no solution.

It is said that the world has become smaller, but wasn't it already small in the remote ages of antiquity? I more and more think so because of the existence of oceans.

Celebration at Borobodur on completion of UNESCO restoration

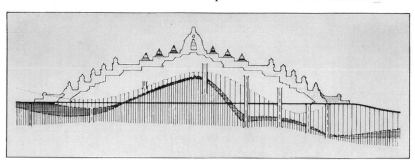

Letter 14

The Dawn of Serenity at Borobudur[62]

Dear Friend,

Dawn. The endless forest of coconut trees is sleeping beneath white mist, while to the east the elegant silhouette of Mount Merapi stands out against a background of golden light. Smoke is rising gently from the volcano. Here and there on the awakening plain below a cock crows and breaks the silence. The lines of stupas stand like silent shadows in the cool of the early morning. Among them I can see the statue of a Buddha facing the rising sun; the new day's light does not seem to disturb his meditation for an instant.

It is the dawn of serenity.

In the half light I can make out a man dressed in white sitting at the foot of the central stupa. A strange vibration emanates from him. I listen. He is murmuring a sutra. Perhaps one of Java's few Buddhists,[63] his hands are joined as he calmly greets the sun that by now is shining on Mount Merapi. Then he goes silently away.

Friend, this is not my first visit to Borobudur. The more I get to know this monument, the more its beauty dazzles me. Some twenty-five years ago UNESCO launched an appeal to the international community to save it. Twenty-seven countries responded and worked with UNESCO and Indonesian experts to move a million stones over a ten-year period so that this chandi[64] could live again in its original form. Borobudur is an exceptional place. It is not a temple—it has no

[62] Reprinted with stylistic modifications from UNESCO *Courier*, July-August, 1994, pp. 68-73.

[63] The Javanese converted to Islam in the 15th century.

[64] A name given to Indonesia's oldest monuments.

place for worship or for making offerings—but a huge Buddhist sanctuary that is both a stupa[65] and a mandala (a cosmic image).

In eighth-century Java the rulers of the prosperous Sailendra (*saila indra*: king of the mountains) dynasty converted to Mahayana[66] Buddhism, a form of Buddhism that came into being around the same time as the beginning of the Christian era. Using the most advanced techniques available, they built this brilliantly designed stone mandala some time around the year 800. Thousands of laborers, craftsmen and artists worked on it. But how brief was the life-span of their masterpiece! Less than a century after its completion Borobudur had disappeared into oblivion, rather like the earth mandala in ancient India that returned to dust after seven days of use.

Why did the dynasty, which had built other masterpieces in central Java, abandon it in the tenth century and turn its attention to the eastern part of the island? Could it have been because of an eruption of Mount Merapi and the violent earthquake that would have followed? Like Pompeii beneath its shroud of ash, Borobudur fell into a thousand-year sleep. It was not until 1814 that an agent rediscovered the legendary chandi, buried deep in the jungle. He had been sent out by Sir Thomas Stamford Raffles, the British governor of Java.

§

Let us take a closer look at Borobudur. On the Kedu plain, formerly known as the garden of Java, the sanctuary stands on the top of a decapitated hill and is built of andesite, a bluish-gray volcanic rock. It is a colossal pyramid of superimposed tiers that are crowned by an enormous bell-shaped stupa. From a distance you can tell that the whole construction is organized around this stupa.

At closer range you can see a heavy stone encasement around the base that was probably built to shore up the monument during its construction. It hides the real base or "hidden foot," which is decorated with 160 reliefs, all of which were photographed shortly after they were discovered in the late nineteenth century

These "invisible" reliefs depict the Sphere of the Desires that the human being is bound to, the *kāmādhātu*. I do not agree with theories that claim this part of the monument was deliberately covered up for religious motives to prevent pilgrims from seeing it. On the one hand,

---

[65] A reliquary or commemorative monument.
[66] A Sanskrit word meaning "a great means of progression" or "Great Vehicle."

the "hidden foot" contains unfinished reliefs indicating that work suddenly came to a halt due to some unexpected event. On the other, as I shall explain later, such an error seems quite inconceivable in such a carefully planned monument. This part of the mandala symbolizes "extreme exteriority:" each side has a stairway in the middle, leading up to the monument's highest point.

The main structure of the sanctuary is composed of this foundation and, standing on top of it, five square terraces. The superstructure consists of three circular terraces. This is the basic shape of the mandala: the square, a symbol of the earth, and the circle, symbolizing the sky, combine to produce the number nine, the supreme figure of Buddhism.

The galleries, which have to be visited clockwise to respect the ritual circumambulation, begin on the second terrace. They are lined with 1,300 wonderful bas-reliefs 2,500 meters long. This is *rūpadhatu*, the Sphere of Forms, in which the human being gives up his thirst for desire but keeps his name and form. This immense stone book related Buddha's life as told in the sutras. Nooks located on the outside of the balustrades that surround the galleries each contain a stone Buddha seated cross-legged on a lotus cushion. There are 432 in all.

Next we come to the foot of the upper part of the mandala. Here the view to the outside, hitherto impeded by the balustrades, suddenly opens up, so that one has a sense of spiritual breadth as one enters the *arūpadāhtu*, the Sphere of Formlessness.

In Borobudur the transition from earth to sky, from form to non-form, is made gently. The square form is not rigorously adhered to: the edges around each square terrace jut out and break up the hard right angles, perhaps in an attempt to use architecture to relieve the monotony of the pilgrim's perambulation. Personally I see an intentional transition to the circle. Aerial photos show that the first two terraces are not exactly circular. A slight deformation makes them more like squares! Only the topmost terrace is a perfect circle.

Borobudur's three spheres mark the spiral stages of an ascension that leads the pilgrim up to the stupa of ultimate truth. This central stupa, whose walls are not perforated like those of the others, contains *nothing*: the ultimate point is nothing but emptiness (*sūnyāta*). Buddha himself is hidden. He is there yet not there; he is being and non-being. Each of the seventy-two small stupas with perforated walls that stand on the three terraces contains a statue of the Buddha. His face can only be imperfectly made out through the gaps in the stonework. These gaps are of different shapes and become less numerous as one approaches the central stupa, signifying the Buddha's increasing invisibility. All these Buddhas have the same hand position (*mudrā*): that of the perpetually moving wheel of the Law.

When we reach the summit, we suddenly share the cosmic vision of Mahayana Buddhism. Here the supreme reality is unveiled, light is born! Yes, Borobudur, which shimmers in a thousand colors from morning to night, itself glistens like a huge beacon. The sanctuary's 504 Buddhas face the four points of the compass and embrace the world with merciful, shining eyes. Not only these stupas, but also the nooks in the wall-parapets, the little towers, the smallest parts of the edifice all reach skywards as if to seize the breath of passing clouds.

§

According to this interpretation, Borobudur is the lotus home of the "Great Buddha of Light," who is depicted in a myriad of small, finely carved Buddhas. Dust itself becomes light. As the doctrine of Mahayana Buddhism has it, the one resides in the many, which is itself the manifestation of the one. In the *Gandhavyūha*, the sacred text of Mahayana Buddhism, light is not the enemy of shade: it is the light of the original emptiness, which transcends the opposition between being and nothingness.

Let us now look at the mandala—this esoteric image that aids active meditation of the Buddhist cosmos—formed by Borobudur. Mandalas, whether painted or sculpted, like the statues in the To-ji temple in Kyoto, are always oriented in relation to a central point. Borobudur, which looks out at the four points of the compass while its "heart" is empty, is a perfect illustration of the mandala concept.

In 1930 the French archeologist and architect Henri Parmentier suggested that Borobudur might have been originally conceived as an immense stupa resting on square terraces but that problems of stability forced the builders to rethink the plans for the upper part. This theory was supported by several participants in the international symposium on Borobudur held in Tokyo in 1980, but it seems unacceptable to me. Even if Borobudur underwent minor changes during its construction, the extreme rigor of its design rules out the idea of any such architectural compromise.

§

The mysterious concordance of the numbers one sees at Borobudur is to my mind sufficient proof. As I have said, there are 432 Buddhas on the square terraces and 72 others on the concentric terraces of the upper part. These numbers are not a mere coincidence. Since the stairways divide each of these groups of statues by four, in each case their total number (432 and 72) and the number of each group thus obtained (108 and 18) can be divided by three and nine. In other words, it is clear that the entire structure was conceived as a function of the number three, which symbolizes unity and the square of three, nine, a sacred number in Buddhism.

Another researcher, J. G. DeCasparis, believed that the central stupa crowning the structure was a tenth terrace, corresponding to the ten stages passed through by the bodhisattva ("Buddha-to-be") before reaching the state of Buddhahood. But when Borobudur was built, only six stages were practiced in Java. Surely they are represented in the six square terraces. But how can the transition from the square to the circle be explained?

I had never been entirely happy with any of these interpretations. Then one day I read the *Jūjū shin ron* (Treatise on the Ten Stages of Thought) in which Kūkai, the Japanese Buddhist Grand Master who founded the esoteric Shingon sect at the beginning of the ninth century, expounds his conception of the mandala.

In his eyes the "ascending transformation of the spirit," for which the mandala is the pictorial expression, is effected in nine exoteric (public) stages, followed by a final, esoteric (secret) stage. Could there be any better definition of Borobudur's architectural significance? Starting from the sphere of animal desire, the monk eventually reaches the "spirit laden with mystery" (*Himitsu-shōgon-Shin*), the culminating and hermetic point. The awakening he experiences then transforms the world into light. Was this not the secret that the immense mandala was whispering to us in the early light of dawn?

So is Borobudur a monument of esoteric Mahayana Buddhism? I cannot say so categorically, but I am profoundly convinced that it is.

Let there be no mistake. I am not claiming that Kūkai influenced the building of Borobudur. I am only saying that Borobudur and Kūkai's teachings share a common source. Kūkai himself was initiated into the esoteric doctrine of Shingon (True Word) in China and introduced the first mandala to Japan.

In which year did he return to his country? In 806, at the very time when the Sailendra were building Borobudur on the island of Java. Let us not forget either that the Todaiji, the temple of the Great Buddha in Nara (Japan), the conception of which was based on the same *Gandavyūha* that is illustrated along most of Borobudur's square terraces, was inaugurated in 751, the date when work on the foundations of the Javanese sanctuary is thought to have begun.

§

This apparent coincidence is not confined to Japan and Indonesia. In Ceylon at the same time thousands of monks practiced the same doctrine of Mahayana Buddhism in the monastery of Abhayagiri, which was in permanent contact with China. And to reach China the Sinhalese monks did not cross mountains but the sea!

This is where the maritime Silk Road comes in. It played a decisive role in the story of the meeting of civilizations. It was a speedy route for the exchange of goods and culture between the East and West, perhaps even before there was an overland Silk Road. Many different peoples used it: Indians, Chinese, Greeks, Romans and Arabs, as well as Indonesians. Ceylon was a port of call for those who crossed the Indian Ocean, and once across the Malacca Straits they either made a detour around Singapore or sailed along the coasts of Sumatra and Java before heading northwards for Canton in southern China. The maritime Silk Road eventually stretched from Italy (Rome) to Japan (Nara), uniting the Indian Ocean, the western Pacific, the China Sea, the Red Sea and the Gulf.

Borobudur must be seen in the context of this network of extremely rich and varied maritime exchanges. The seas of Southeast Asia teemed with activity in the seventh and eighth centuries. And when talking about Indo-Javanese civilization, especially a Buddhist monument, we should not forget the part played by cultural influences from nations other than India.

Look carefully at the meditating Buddhas of Borobudur. Their expression differs from that of Indian or Thai statues, and has a greater affinity with those of China and Japan. Did not the Sailendra have a large fleet that travelled to China as well as to India and Ceylon? Moreover the monks of Abhayagiri often stopped in Java on their way to China. They were even reported to have founded a community in the eighth century on a hill near Borobudur.

Could there be a link between the presence of this monastic community and the building of Borobudur? There is no definite proof but the shape of the stupas in Borobudur is not unlike that of the stupas in the lotus style of Anurādhapura, Ceylon's ancient capital. I also remember being struck by the resemblance between two statues of Buddha discovered in the ruins of Abhayagiri and the statues at Borobudur.

It is of course impossible to understand the conception of Borobudur without referring to the local culture. In Indonesia there was a form of ancestor worship that venerated the ancestors' spirits by building tiered pyramids in their honor. Could this great pyramid-shaped mandala have been built without such a tradition? The world owes this unique heritage to the Indonesian people.

The sun has risen over Borobudur. My thoughts turn to the outward-looking spirit of the eighth century. There were no cultural boundaries then. Peoples absorbed each other's cultures like travellers slaking their thirst together. Have those far-off times gone forever? I cannot believe that they have. Down in the water, lotuses communicate with one another through their roots. Dewdrops on petals reflect the same moon that shines down on white flowers thousands of miles apart. And the sun that shines on Mount Merapi once shone on pilgrims' faces at a time when beauty was the splendor of truth.

Borobudur: A Chronology

The site: a vast Mahayana Buddhist monument in the form of a pyramid-shaped mandala, built in the heart of Java around 800 A. D. by the Sailendra dynasty and abandoned shortly after its completion.

Size: the square base, with sides measuring some 120 meters, covers an area of almost one and a half hectares; the central dome that crowns the monument is almost 35 meters above the base.

1814: rediscovery of the monument by Sir Thomas Stamford Raffles, who has the site cleared of rubble and vegetation. Specialists compile documentation based on drawings.

1885: discovery of "the hidden foot"—the original base—and its bas-reliefs concealed behind the retaining wall needed to keep the structure from sliding.

1907—1911: Theodoor Van Erp carries out the first restoration work. He dismantles and rebuilds the three circular terraces and the stupas.

1955: Indonesia seeks UNESCO's advice on measures to prevent the monument's dilapidation.

1972: UNESCO launches an international appeal to save Borobudur.

1975—1982: restoration work carried out.

February 23, 1983: inaugural ceremony to mark the completion of restoration work. Total cost: $20 million, two-thirds from the Indonesian government and $7 million from UNESCO's international campaign, in which 27 countries took part.

1991: Borobudur included on UNESCO's World Heritage list.

Ship-shaped roofs of the Toradja with the outer pillar
Figurines standing on the balcony below the entrance to a grave

Letter 15

The Riddle of the Toradja

Dear Friend,

I had wanted for a number of years to know more about the mythical Kingdom of Toradja. The Toradja people build and live in huge boat-shaped houses in the mountains of the island of Sulawesi (Celebes). They are, indeed, a people wrapped in mystery. On the occasion of my second visit to Borobudur in Java, I finally had the opportunity of visiting this Toradja community, which looks as if history forgot it. I found we could fly to Ujunpandang at the southern extremity of Sulawesi, if we start from Denpasar on Bali at six in the morning.

At Ujunpandang we hunt up a jeep and head north along the west coast toward the legendary kingdom. In about ten hours, we are going to enter a rugged mountainous region. Already it is completely dark as we creep along the mountain path; our headlights illuminate only a white fog. Now our bodies shiver in a chill in this southern country at night. I happen to have a bottle of whiskey; never before has it tasted so good. When the car suddenly stops, we can make out clearly, even in the deep darkness, the outline of the buildings that jut their gigantic horns into the air. We come to our hotel, which is shaped like a Toradja house. We are in Rampateo, the central village of the Toradja people.

The Toradjas are centered here and their villages dot the neighboring valleys. One feels that one is visiting such a settlement while in the National Museum of Ethnology in Osaka. But the actual size of the Toradja houses is twice that of those we see in the museum and the same size as the Japanese houses called *gasshozukuri* (which means with roofs as steep as hands clasped in prayer). In Japan, houses of this style are found only in Shirakawa village in the mountain area of Gifu Prefecture and are classified by UNESCO as a world heritage.

The shapes of the roofs of the Toradja houses are said to have the form of a ship. A special pillar placed outside supports each end of the horn-shaped roof (symbolic of shamanism). On the facades of such houses there are wonderful carvings. The raised floors are characteristic of some other architecture in the South Seas, and the wooden pillars are so exquisite they remind one of the great platform of Kiyomizu Temple in Kyoto.

Near each such residence where an extended family lives, there is a granary. This is a little smaller than the house, but it has the same shape of roof and differs only in the form of its pillars. Rodents can not climb the smooth columns. The main item stored there is not the famous coffee but rice. The way of making rice paddies here in Toradja does not differ at all from ancient Japan when we substitute the Japanese ox for water buffalo.

If we were looking for the original form of the Japanese house as exemplified in the Ise Shrine, it would be correct to say that almost all the same elements are present in the construction of Toradja houses. The Japanese architectural form spoken of as the "basic Yamato style" or the "unique God-style" is exemplified in the granary called, "The Imperial Rice Storehouse" at the Ise shrine. Its style of arranging pillars and using straight lines closely resembles the structure of the Toradja storehouse. Only the roofs differ. The simple, straight lines of Ise are not found in Toradja architecture

However there are straight lines in the roofs of the Buginese who are neighbors of the Toradja. Moreover, the Buginese cross straight rafters to form all the ornamental crossing points which are found on the oblique crossing logs (called *chigi*) of the Ise shrine ridgepole. Also on top of Buginese houses are horizontal cigar-shaped logs (*katsuogi*). In brief, with regard to roofs and roof-supporting pillars, Ise appears to be a synthesis of the pillars of Toradja and the roofs of the Buginese. Besides, even though the roofs at Ise have the straight-line form, elsewhere in Japan some of the clay figures (*haniwa*) that have turned up in archeological digs dating from the Tumulus (ancient tomb) Period of 250—552 show roofs with the curvilinear outline of ships.

§

The most amazing thing about the Toradjas is their funerals. After our jeep has followed a narrow path until we reach the village of Remo, it becomes apparent that innumerable holes have been cut in the face of the cliff. When we draw near, we realize that these are square grave holes. And below each hole a balcony has been made. There, robed in white are mummy-like objects, erect and standing in a row with both arms outstretched toward the village. These figures are not as ghoulish a sight as you might expect. In fact, these effigies called *tau-tau* are not the dead but apparitions of the dead. Their large immovable eyes seem to look into the empty air as though they are guarding the living.

When I saw that sight, my thoughts rushed across southern seas to the *moai* on Easter Island. Standing on this lonely island of the South Pacific are these huge stone statues that must have been constructed for some purpose. However, that purpose remains a mystery. What flashed back to me, however, was the eyes of the *moai*. There are no eyeballs in the *moai* on display in the *Musée de l'homme* in Paris or in other museums, but the *moai* once had eyeballs. These unusual figures now have the eyes strangely hollowed. For a long time people thought that the statues originally were made this way, but recently while a man was trying to raise a *moai* that had fallen over, he found a white coral lump in the rubble below the statue. When he placed it in the *moai's* empty socket, it suddenly snapped snugly into place. And, in addition, he also found a black stone that served as the eye's pupil. Now a number of *moai* stand up with their eyes wide open.

When I saw the eyes of the Toradja dolls, I intuitively knew, "These are the eyes of the *moai*." The expression of the eyes is the same. Also, the heads of the dolls of Toradja are wrapped with white turbans. These remind one of the caps worn by the *moai* after they are restored. Perhaps here lies the solution to the puzzle of the huge statues on far-away Easter Island.

The *moai* are not just commemorative statues for departed kings. They are the apparitions of the souls of the dead. After their death, they stand there with their large eyes to watch over the living. Indeed, when we think in such a way, we understand why the *moai* are not facing the sea but are looking inland.

§

Friend, when anyone dies in Toradja they do not immediately have a funeral. The dead person is enshrined in a "provisional hut" so as to spend a short time with the living. Their burial awaits the next harvest time. And the family will spend their whole fortune on a funeral performed in the fall when all the villagers gather. The heads of water buffalo are struck off at one stroke of a great sword, and several hogs are also sacrificed. It is an event for the whole village; it seems just like a festival. Then a ladder is set up against the cliff wall, and some people carry the coffin of the deceased to the family grave hole. A new *tau-tau* resembling this deceased person is placed in front of the grave high on the balcony. For an individual Toradja, the funeral is, indeed, the greatest ceremony of one's whole life. In one place, I saw that logs had been driven into the cliff to form a shelf for the coffin. This form of burial is also seen in South China. Moreover, Toradja graves are not limited to holes dug in the cliffs. They also utilize natural caves. In these, the coffins of many centuries accumulate.

§

Now, speaking of the provisional funeral, we must notice that this kind of funeral was used in ancient Japan. Even today, in "private" and "regular"[67] funerals, this tradition is carried forward. In the old chronicle, *Kojiki*, there is the clearest account of the stories associated with the practices of those ancient days. The most seminal of these stories concerns Izanagi and Izanami, a kind of Adam and Eve among the gods—the "creative couple of Japan" in Papinot's words. The last child born to this couple was the god of fire. The birth caused Izanami's death. When Izanagi yearned for and sought to visit the wife whose death he had indirectly brought about, the place he arrived at was certainly the mansion *mogari* (preliminary hut).[68] Izanami had already fallen victim to putrefaction, and maggots and snakes were coming out of her body.[69] Izanami was angry because Izanagi saw her

---

[67] The private, preliminary, or informal funeral (*missō*) is for close family only. The regular or formal funeral (*honsō*) is public and held with greater ceremony.

[68] In this context, *mogari* may be thought of as a kind of antechamber to the domain of complete and final death.

[69] Compare the epic of Gilgamesh, which some consider the oldest of all written stories, dating perhaps two or three millennia before the time of Christ. In it there are similar grim details from the land of the dead where Gilgamesh

like that and because he had run after her. Izanagi, after fleeing from there, had to cleanse himself in a river as soon as possible. The custom still remains in Okinawa of drinking and dancing while circling around the dead, perhaps in remembrance of Izanagi's visit to Izanami. Funeral feasting, if not dancing, is practiced all over the area extending from the Kyoto-Osaka region into central Japan.

As Kunio Yanagita, the famous ethnologist, points out, "In Japan the spirits of the dead linger for a while in their place of lifetime abode." But this is something fundamentally different from both the Christian belief in which the soul just separated from its dead body is at once called into the Kingdom of God and the Buddhist belief in which the soul starts quickly for the Pure Land of Buddha.[70] For me, there is an invisible thread between far-away Toradja and Japan in that on both sides it is thought that the spirits of the dead dwell for a time with the living, and that, therefore, a dual system of funeral services is appropriate. This system requires there to be a "temporary" funeral ceremony leading eventually to the regular and final one. In the period of ancient tombs (3rd to the 7th century), we Japanese had our main funeral service, like the Toradja people, in the fall after harvest.

The tradition of extreme respect for the dead during the Tumulus Period ends in 686 with the imperial funeral of Emperor Temmu. That funeral lasted two years, and the imperial palace itself became a mansion of *mogari*. If we look carefully at that time, we see that Buddhist monks were not allowed to conduct a service in the palace so they had to perform it at their own temple. But after this Buddhism gradually permeated both the government and the general populace, and the idea of a world after death, as in Christianity, was introduced. With the popularization of this idea and of cremation, the period of great tombs comes to an end.

The imperial funeral that was originally the tradition of Japan, was revived after twelve centuries on the occasion of the funeral of Emperor

---

finds his beloved friend Enkidu who tells him that his body is dropping away like a piece of old clothing, soon to be filled with dust. In the *Kojiki* Izanami says to Izanagi, "Why did you want to see me in this form?" In facing the reality of death, at one point Gilgamesh is assured that the dead can never join the living and that only the living can join the dead.

[70] In Japanese, *hotoke* refers primarily to the Buddha and secondarily to the deceased.

Meiji. Prior to this, the emperors did not receive the lavish imperial funerals performed in Europe, but now they were accorded what was in effect a revival of the earlier Japanese funereal archetype.

§

Friend, my thoughts here fly toward Canada 10,000 kilometers away.

The time was 1989 when I went to Vancouver. As I was waiting for a man at the airport, suddenly someone tapped me on the shoulder. When I turned around, who could it be but Nuburi Toko! Fifteen years earlier he had received great acclaim for putting on a performance in Paris as leader of the Yūkara Theatre. Yūkara is an ancient Ainu epic orally transmitted from generation to generation. Toko made it accessible to the public by putting it into dramatic form and thus making it visible. He was then invited to Canada to spend five years producing the "Garden of the Gods" as a master carving. Toko said to me, "I was just thinking it would be nice to have Hattori here when, at this precise moment, you appeared in front of me!" Having rejoiced at our chance meeting, we promised to meet again in a couple of days after we had each returned to our respective jobs.

Two days later he took me to a native Canadian restaurant. There we were able to hear a variety of interesting things from a charming young Canadian Indian woman seated next to me. On this evening the relationship of the Toradja tribe and the Ainu people was the topic of discussion. It was significant because in this chance way was disclosed an invisible thread connecting these widely separated Canadian Indians with their possible cultural cousins.

The theories of Takeshi Umehara that the Ainu are no other than the people who created the Jōmon culture (12,000 B.C.—400 B.C.) and that they arrived from the north and from the south, seem to me to be well-established.[71] The argument which seeks to refute his first theory states that the masks seen on the earthen figures of the Jōmon period are not a part of Ainu custom. But that argument alone is not enough to persuade me. What I would like to pay more attention to is the motifs and colors of the carvings.

---

[71] The author of the article on Japan in *Encarta*, the Microsoft electronic encyclopedia, accepts Umehara's theory. "The Jōmon's descendants are the Ainu, a tribal people who may have populated all the Japanese islands in the 2nd and 1st millennia B.C."

The three colors of the Toradja carvings are dark red, black, and yellow. These are identical to the three colors of the Ainu. And what about the Canadian Indians? In several of their locations, the same colors predominate with the addition only of green.

Next are the motifs. Conspicuous for the Toradja are the owl and the form of waves. Similarly, the Ainu deity Kotankoro Kamui is the owl, and the main motifs of embroidery on clothing are waves and killer whales. The same interest in bears that is manifested among the Ainu shows up in Canadian totems. Here on the totem pole displayed in the restaurant, I saw placed at the top the great eagle or raven to represent the souls of ancestors, and, on the lower part, a huge fish. On other totems I saw the bear.

When I asked the young Indian lady in the restaurant about the meaning of the fish, I heard her say, "*Kelawa.*" As I did not understand, I asked her to write it on a sheet of paper. She wrote, "Killer whale." And she informed us that here Indians deeply respect nature, as do the Ainu people. I might add that the living things from which we get our food are all subjects of prayer for the Ainu, especially in the ceremony dedicated to the Akiaji or Fall Tasting. These rites are actually a kind of memorial service or mass for the living beings that are becoming food for human beings. Now let us revisit the Toradja people.

Friend, it is said that in remote antiquity the Toradja people drifted by ocean currents from southern China or Indochina to the Celebes. They could not abandon the thought of some day returning to their land of origin. First they were living near their wrecked ships. Then they built and lived in houses on the shoreline, houses that were shaped like boats to remind them of their journeying by sea. With the arrival of the Buginese, the Toradjas were driven away from their coastal homes. They then went more and more deeply into the heart of the mountains to construct their houses. The mountain houses emanate the same feeling of nostalgia. Similar phenomena are observed in tribes on the shore of Kamui Lake in Sumatra. I presume these tribes share the same origin.

The removal of peoples in these ways is not limited to the history of the tribes on Celebes or Sumatra. The phenomenon occurs in various countries of the world including Japan. An example from yet another part of the world concerns Maghreb[72] in North Africa where we encounter the blond Berbers. This people, who now live in the Atlas mountain range, also dwelt at first on the coastline. Prior to the Christian era Phoenicians drove them from the coast. Later they again retreated because of the arrival of the Arabs. In short, they had to remove their dwelling places into an inhospitable mountain zone. It is becoming more and more difficult to reconstitute the memories of these people.

However, for the Toradja people there is something much more decisively indicative of their origins even than the shape of their roofs. It is the shape of their coffins. Because of the missionary activities of the Society of Jesus, all recent ones have taken on the Christian shape, but the older ones are boat-shaped coffins whether they are done in stone or wood. On the other hand, concerning the ancient funeral services of the Ainu we hardly know anything. The reason is that they were persecuted and oppressed for two thousand years by our Japanese predecessors, escaping farther and farther north. We can hardly imagine that it would be possible for them to conserve their total heritage as Ainu. How did their coffins come to be shaped as they were? When I asked Nuburi Toko about this, he closed his eyes for a while and then said: "Now I recall when I was a child. My grandmother had died, and the straw mats in which she was wrapped were boat shaped. My mother told me that her shroud was fixed like this because she would be going to a far country."

Invisible threads connect diverse peoples in countries distant from each other. It is impossible for me to concede that all these similarities might be laughed off as due only to coincidence. Perhaps the ones who laugh do not know that long ago Indonesians traversed the Indian Ocean to become the present inhabitants of Madagascar. On this island off the southeast coast of Africa, when time literally did not yet know history, there were large outrigger boats of the type that Indonesians had used in crossing over the raging waves of the Indian Ocean. Viewed from the front these boats look like spiders. In the pre-Christian era, the Greeks saw them at least as far west as the Red Sea.

---

[72]The ethnic groups of this ancient region are the Berbers and Arabs. According to the electronic reference, *The American Heritage Talking Dictionary* (1995), Maghreb is a "region of northwest Africa comprising the coastlands and the Atlas Mountains of Morocco, Algeria, and Tunisia."

On this same island of Madagascar there is an important ceremony referred to in French as the ceremony of *retournement* (meaning a complete change from the provisional to the eternal). This indicates that the dead were temporarily buried. After about a year the bodies were exhumed and the burial clothing was changed to make ready for the formal funeral. The belief is that at this time the deceased finally entered into the sleep of eternity.

In Indonesia, I found the elusive Kingdom of Toradja that I longed to know. It is the authentic source for so much in today's Madagascar.

Letter 16

A Culture of Death, a Culture of Life

Dear Friend,

As I recall, Alain the philosopher[73] expressed himself in this way: "When you handle sand at the seashore and let it fall smoothly, a cone will emerge. That is one of the most stable forms in nature. Pyramids have that same conical angle. In them lies the tranquillity of eternal death. . . ."

My esteemed Professor Michitairō Tanaka of Kyoto University, the rigorous Greek scholar, once stepped outside his chosen specialty to give us the following beautiful depiction: "There is a narrow window on the descent from a pyramid's side toward the royal chamber at the center. Once every sixteen years for a period of only three days, light streams through that window from the star Sirius and falls on the royal coffin. Then, in that light, the face of the Pharaoh is seen to be faintly smiling . . . ."

Isn't this the portrayal of a strange and mysterious culture of death? Many people consider that Egypt had a culture of death and that, in contrast to it, a culture of life was born in Greece. Certainly if we look at the three huge pyramids of Giza (modern Al-Jīzah)—Khufu, Khafre, and Menkaure, with their desert background of reddish brown—even a file of camels appears as a file of ants, and we feel as though the great Death looms silently.

But was the culture of Egypt a culture of death? This question became insistent in my mind, not thirty years ago when I visited Giza, but at a different and very remote place. That was in 1980 when I was

---

[73] "Alain" is the pseudonym of Émile-Auguste Chartier (1868—1951), a French philosopher who, according to Britannica's *Micropaedia*, "profoundly influenced several generations of readers."

first visiting the terra cotta army of the first emperor of China, Qin Shihuang Di,[74] in the suburbs of Xian.

Some years earlier, while a farmer was digging a well in this area, he happened upon a heap of fragments of strange and wonderful terra cotta figures. The conclusion in the report of the archeological experts who went to the site was that these were fragments of the funeral figurines of a satellite tomb of the Qin emperor. This first report was in 1974. What has come to view since the excavations began—the buried figures of First Emperor's retainers and cavalry—has created as great a stir as the archeological event of the discovery by Howard Carter of Tutankhamen's tomb in 1922. In the vast area of the original find near Xian were 6,000 figures of men with horses, each life-sized and unique in appearance. It is now said that the total number of figurines, including those in the fourth pit, comes to 8,000.

When I went to Xian, the Great Cultural Revolution and the conviction and sentencing of the Gang of Four were events of the recent past. At last China's heavy door began to be opened by Deng Xiaoping. At the excavation site, I saw a breathtaking scene. As if symbolizing the rise of the Qin in western China and their conquest of the six eastern kingdoms, the army corps stands facing east, assembled in a square battle array and lined up in perfect order. Placed among the soldiers are horses pulling battle chariots. The warriors who shoot their catapults are either standing or sitting at their stations. At the time of my visit, the soldiers discovered in the rear part of the pit had not yet been excavated.

The satellite tomb containing the burial figures of these soldiers is located 1.5 kilometers to the east of the first imperial tomb. After viewing what had so far been excavated and the objects in the repair and reconstruction studio, I spoke with the director of the museum that covers the excavated site.

"Am I not correct that, if we credit Chinese tradition, buried treasure was not only on one side of the imperial tombs but on all four sides? Don't you think that there would be something on the western side, since there is so much on the east?" The director promptly agreed, saying, "I think so. However, so far we have lacked the time and money to investigate."

---

[74] Referred to hereafter as the Qin emperor or as First Emperor, which is the literal translation of "Shihuang Di."

That was in July of 1980, and in November of that year a friend who was in Paris as a Chinese diplomat in the permanent delegation made an excited telephone call to me. "Hattori, you were right! A different army has been discovered on the west. Moreover, it isn't all terra cotta; there are bronze figures!" Later he sent photographs of fragments of bronze vehicles as they were excavated. These are now fully restored.

The imperial tomb proper has not been opened, but the Annals of History[75] depicts how the tomb was constructed: First Emperor "set about the construction of his own imperial tomb as soon as he ascended the throne. 700,000 workers were conscripted, and a tunnel that reached the underground palace (the main tomb) was dug breaking through the water strata three times. The one hundred or so rooms of the palace were filled with treasures and anyone attempting to get to it was shot to death by an automatic arrow-shooting device. In the royal chamber, under a blue sky inlaid in gold and silver to imitate the heavenly bodies, were both rivers (the Yellow and the Yangtze) made of mercury and flowing into the great ocean. In the center the imperial coffin was enshrined." The description goes on to say that a perpetual lamp was lit using the oil of a beautiful "mermaid." Surely this is a mistake for "whale"! And, lastly, there are the words, "Furthermore, around the imperial tomb were arranged his imperial guards."

If we understand the fact that the last line I've quoted from this ancient description relates to the great army of 8,000 terra-cotta figures, then we must conclude that the above-mentioned description must be exact and without exaggeration. The emperor's tomb is probably 50 times larger than this satellite tomb.

There is no reason to doubt that what the Qin emperor deeply desired was immortality. For its sake he ordered that a study be made of the beliefs and practices of the mountain hermits of Taoism. He sent Xufu to Japan to seek the elixir of immortality and eternal youthfulness. Japan was thought of as a utopia where Taoists thought the immortals live. The underground palace was an architectural expression of the emperor's vow. Everything necessary for the emperor in eternal life was supposed to be there. The designs of the interior of this imperial tomb can be guessed from the tombs of a later period such

---

[75] The Annals of History is by the greatest historian of the Han Dynasty, Ssu-ma Ch'ien (c. 145—c. 85).

as the Tang Dynasty (618—903) or, again, from the thirteen Ming tombs of a still later period (1368-1644). This is because the tomb of the Qin emperor is considered to represent a revolution in tomb style that continued to be used throughout the various dynasties that followed.

About 50 miles northwest of Xian in what I am inclined to call the Valley of the Kings, there are a total of a hundred and seventy ancient tomb sites. These are tombs from the Tang dynasty (618—c. 907). Not yet opened is the tomb of the second Tang emperor, Taizong. Also unopened is the tomb of Wu Zetien, who as consort succeeded the third Tang emperor, Gaozong, upon his death and was buried in the same tomb with him. There are many mounds for their retainers. The medium-sized ones, such as the tomb of Prince Yi De and that of Imperial Princess Yong Tai, have been opened. Her coffin, which can be reached by descending a tunnel, is adorned with frescoes of court ladies like the grave in Takamatsu-zuka, an ancient tomb (7th century A.D.) south of Nara in Japan. The coffin is placed under a blue sky with sun, moon, and constellations. There are also drawings of a blue dragon on the east and a white tiger on the west. There are chambers filled with pots for grain and figurines of domestic animals. These have all been passed down from the Qin dynasty (221 B.C.—206 B.C.) to the Han (roughly 206 B.C.—220 A.D.) and from the Sui (589—618) to the Tang (618—907). During much of this time Xian was the capital. In the municipal museum in the city of Xianyang[76] there are 3,000 smaller painted burial figures of troops and horses from the Han dynasty that had overthrown the Qin. Burial figures steadily decrease in size and number as the periods advance, which suggests that prayer for eternal life was turning into a mere formality.

§

I am probably not the only person who, after visiting these imperial tombs, is moved to ask, "Isn't this the pyramids all over again?" What I noticed here was the layout of this necropolis (underground palace of the dead) not the form of its exterior mound.

---

[76] Xianyang (Hsien-yang), on the north bank of the Wei River, is about 12 miles northwest of Xian "in an area that was the cradle of early Chinese civilization," according to *Micropaedia.* Its importance began with the rise of the Qin state.

connected? We need to pay increasing attention to any ancient book like the Book of the Dead that contains essentially the same ideas about death, whether it appears in the Tibet of southwest China or in Egypt. How should we explain this fact? Such questions are not quickly answered.

Almost all Chinese imperial tombs use natural mountains. In a circular mountain, a tunnel is dug from its side to the underground palace, and in front of that palace, on the earth's surface, stood several rectangular buildings which have since disappeared. In other words, the shape of the tomb complex is a keyhole. A similar design is found in Japan in the ancient tomb period, 3rd to 7th century.

Once I thought in this way: "Isn't it a rather natural idea to use a mountain for a tomb? If one goes about constructing a mountain in a desert that has no mountains, the result is a pyramid. Perhaps even the thought of an underground palace was one born in China and brought over to Egypt from there. In that case, there is in the area around Tibet, which has a Book of the Dead, something that becomes the missing link to unite Egypt and China . . . ."

The Book of the Dead even came across to Japan, but the similarities between the Egyptian Book of the Dead and the main points of the Book of the Dead in Tibet are too close to be explained away as due to mere chance. For example, the dead cross the river of Hades in a boat and reach another shore to be judged. In the pyramids and in the Valley of the Kings many remains of "boats of the dead" have been found.

However, when we think in this way, the order of historical periods becomes an insuperable problem. The time when the Egyptian pyramids appeared was around 2500 B.C.,[77] and this kind of tomb was not seen in China until the third century B.C. tomb of the first Qin emperor. Therefore, Egypt could not have derived its idea from Chinese tombs that were constructed so long after the Egyptian pyramid-building period. Accomplishments of the Qin tribe can hardly be documented back to the 7th century B.C. The great Qin emperor came to power only in the 3rd century B.C. Therefore, we must not think of the stream of influence as flowing from East to West but from West to East. There is one fact that makes this idea a powerful one for

---

[77] One of the most famous of the pyramids, the Pyramid of Khafre, was built around 2530 B.C.

me. Egypt's being known to China from remote antiquity makes sense because of the walkway to a Tang Dynasty Qianling Mausoleum which shows exactly the same figures of reclining goats as adorn the Temple of Karnak on the bank of the Nile.

"If that's the case, when we retrace the periods of history, we may find that the model for the first Chinese emperor's tomb was the Egyptian pyramid. Therefore, the shape of the artificial mountain is that of a quadrilateral pyramid even if it is a little too flat. That indicates, I think, that the First Emperor had the idea of a pyramid but had never actually seen one—or even a picture of one. Nomads transfer information orally and not pictorially. That underground palace was the pharaoh's mansion of eternal life!"

This thought germinated in my mind, and soon changed into a firm conviction. However, it took a long time to confirm such an audacious hypothesis. For me, the problem was whether any roads were open to the West at that time. Usually it is agreed that the Silk Road (a road to the West), began in 139 B.C. when the Han Emperor Wudi sent to Ferghana[78] a certain Zhang Qian who at that time opened the northern Tien Shan route. The mission of Zhang Qian was to ally the Kushans, who then lived in Ferghana, to the Han. Then the Huns could be attacked from both East and West. We must somehow fill in a vacuum of approximately one century between the Qin emperor and Wudi.

However, in due time I noticed an important fact. The history of the Silk Road reported in the Chinese records as having begun with Zhang Qian's journey is history only from the Chinese point of view. What was the situation as seen from the Persian side? In other words, how would the Silk Road appear when thought about as a route not running *to* the West but *from* the West? The problem is that although there are records of many Chinese events there are no documents from Persia. How can we resolve this problem? The answer is to look at the cultural artifacts.

I would like to note here that the military groups of the Qin dynasty artistically embodied in the burial figures of horses and men were a mixed assemblage. There are men who are clearly the ones thought of as Huns and north-China barbarians—*Hu* people. As for the figures of the horses and men, it is inferred from them that Chinese soldiers adopted both the costumes of the Hu, the jackets worn by the horse-

---

[78] Today raw silk is one of Ferghana's products.

adopted both the costumes of the Hu, the jackets worn by the horse-riding people of Iran, and their foreign equestrian strategy of shooting arrows from horseback.

Many assume that *Hu* means the Persians. Even more people realize it refers to Iranians because the term *Iranian* is more inclusive than *Persian*. For example, the Kushans of Ferghana are included in the connotation of *Iranian*. The previously referred to Emperor Wudi tried to ally himself with the Kushans and sought to cut off the Huns' access to the West. This means that Wudi already knew that beyond the Tien Shan mountain range lay the birthplace of "heavenly horses": the region of Ferghana and, specifically, the city of Samarkand.

Right from the start of their little kingdom, the Qin people loved horses. Even earlier, the kings of the Zhou (Chou)[79] valued horses and allowed the Qin tribe to keep them at the confluence of two rivers. And that same Qin dynasty little by little proved the power of their mobility during the Spring and Autumn period (8th – 5th century B.C.) and the succeeding period of Warring States (5th – 3rd century). The Qin was one of six competing dynasties. Under the First Emperor the Qin dynasty won out over the others and gradually replaced the Western Zhou (1122—770). I think that the horse played an important role in this development. The Qin became a horse-riding military group.

Furthermore, among the excavated artifacts in the satellite tomb of the First Emperor we can see patterns that clearly show Scythian[80] animal motifs. And the Scythians were much admired as skilled horse-riding people themselves. The Wei River near Xianyang where the Qin raised horses is just west of Ch'ang-an which later became a terminus of the Silk Road. I would risk asserting that some threads connected this terminus with the Scythians who lived on the Caspian seacoast. However, was it only with the Scythians? Here my thoughts at last found their way to the Achaemenid Dynasty of Persia. That dynasty conquered the whole area in the period from around the 6th to the 5th century B.C.

---

[79] Zhou (combining the Western and Eastern phases) dynasty dates are ?1122—c. 256.

[80] The Scythians were called Sacae in classical sources. Their art emphasized real and mythical animals, including anthropomorphic beasts. They were masters of equestrian warfare.

King Darius the First (also known as Darius the Great, b. 550—d. 486) created the "king's roads" in every direction using the horse-riding tactics brought to him by the Scythians, and he won control not merely over the whole area from Mesopotamia to Egypt and the eastern Mediterranean. His southern route of conquest extended even to northwest India and the Indus River; and his northern route, to Sogdiana (Samarkand) in central Asia. The whole of what we call Western Turkestan[81] was under his power. A step to the east is Eastern Turkestan, present-day Xinjiang Uygur. All this was known as "Xiyu" (western regions) in Han China. In that long ago time, the Turkish Road passed freely through this vast territory. It is said that lapis lazuli and rubies were carried from Sogdiana to Egypt. Furthermore, Darius the Great also opened the road from Egypt to the Indus, and he may have connected the mouth of the Nile with the Red Sea by means of a canal. He was the first emperor to be convinced that it is trade that brings prosperity to a nation. His military corps, that was a mixture of infantry and cavalry, moved rapidly on these royal highways. And, about a hundred years later, Alexander the Macedonian followed this road system of Darius.

There is something we should pay attention to. At this time the Persian Empire already extended from Egypt to the region of Sogdiana; moreover, it is a fact that information, news, and intelligence were flowing freely because of the commerce that used the network of roads with caravan-*sarai* (relay stations). Therefore, in Darius' sphere of influence, even the wonders of Egypt must have been generally known west of the Tien Shan range.

Darius' army did not cross the Tien Shan. However, what about the nomads of the north? We can readily think that peoples of the same racial stock would be going and coming all across the broad expanse of Turkestan and would necessarily be exchanging information with whomever they met. It is not unnatural even to think that by means of the nomads who galloped about on their horses, news of the Achaemenid Dynasty of Persia was reaching China. The question is whether there was someone who could efficiently use such information. And, if so, would we not be correct in assuming that the First Emperor of the Qin was that one?

---

[81] Turkestan (or Turkistan) is a region of Central Asia. Its western part lay in the former Soviet Union and is now Kyrgyzstan, Tajikistan, Uzbekistan, and Turkmenistan. Its eastern part is the Xinjiang region of China.

Whenever a lot of reflection of this kind occurs, understanding is born. To begin with, as we look at the Chinese imperial terra cotta army, we can visualize military units composed of a mixture of walking and riding soldiers (who are characteristic of Darius' army), Hu style clothes (Persian clothing), imperial highways on which war chariots could move swiftly in all directions (compare the king's roads under Darius), irrigation (Persian *kalez*), the establishment of a currency system, and enormous buildings. In this process of looking and imagining, we can suddenly comprehend that the comparison often made between the Qin Empire and Rome happens only because of an ignorant neglect of Persia. If Persia had not existed, all these comparisons between Rome and China might not have existed either. As it actually turned out, Rome learned from Greece, and Greece learned from Persia.

The empire of Alexander of the 4th century B.C. almost completely coincides with the map of Darius' empire (of the 6th – 5th century). It's just a matter of leaders having been replaced. The square battle formation (phalanx) is the formation Alexander had used in Persia before its adoption by the Qin in China. In fact Greece under Alexander imitated many systems of Achaemenid Persia. Also the mixture of races progressed. Persians appointed Greeks as equals, and by the same token, Greeks did not despise Persians. Alexander passed along the roads of Darius and was advancing on foot to the region of Sogdiana. This Greek Empire split and collapsed, and the nation of Bactria in front of the Pamirs[82] was born at just about the time of the First Emperor of Qin. Bactria[83] certainly flourished as a relay point on the Silk Road. Consequently, at this time there was nothing to obstruct the East-West flow of information.

§

Friend, when we come to think this way, there is an exceedingly strong possibility that the idea of eternal life symbolized in the

---

[82] The Pamirs, also referred to as Pamir, constitute the high plateau where the Hindu Kush, Tien Shan, and Himalayan mountain ranges converge. This glacial valley lies in present-day Tajikistan, just north of Afghanistan and Pakistan.

[83] Bactria, an ancient country of West Asia, was located between the Oxus River (modern Amu Darya) and the Hindu Kush Mountains.

pyramids of Egypt reached the young Qin emperor via the roads of Darius as well as those of Alexander. The unusual big fellow painted and described in the records as having a strange physiognomy and prominent nose possessed the very features of the First Emperor. There are even rumors that the Qin emperor was not a legitimate child as well as other rumors that his features were suggestive of some of the northern people, but aside from these matters, what I would like to emphasize is that he introduced Western knowledge and strategy, especially the mobility of troops, despite the fact that he possessed only bronze weapons while his enemies used iron. I wish also to suggest that he probably got his idea of "Empire" from the West, including territorial consolidation and bureaucratic organization. These also benefited both the Greeks and Persians.

Friend, this kind of hypothesis will surely repel a certain group of people. My thinking is as follows. Until now history has been written too much from the point of view of one country. In the later books of history written about the Qin, only the eastward military expeditions of the First Emperor are recorded. For the Chinese who dwelt in "the East," the West and North contained barbarians. On the other hand, in the West people still tend to limit the origin of Europe to Greece and Rome and perhaps also the Judeo-Christian heritage. According to this ethnocentric point of view, all of Central Asia became a complete blank once and for all.

The Egyptians and Persians influenced Europe before the Greeks. After Rome's dominant time, Arabs influenced Europe. But there are few people who feel the intrinsic value and vitality of these other civilizations. Perhaps this is because of the powerful, exclusivistic religions of Judaism and Christianity. Islam occupied Central Asia, extending as far as Persia (present-day Iran, Iraq, and Turkey). I have to think this fact is relevant to the tendency in the Occident to minimize the cultural histories of this area.

Once Central Asia was the center of history. The fact that it was the main artery of East-West civilizational interchange means that we must look again at this area from a comprehensive, historical perspective. Because of Sogdiana, which Kyuzo Katō the Japanese steppe route specialist has emphasized, we may even think that the road through it is the one along which the souls of the pharaohs passed.

§

Friend, I've just now understood that what characterized Egypt was not "a culture of death" but "a culture of life." The Egyptians did not worship death but prayed for eternal life and resurrection: By *a prayer for life after death the goddess Isis called back from Hades her husband Osiris. The very thing that was cherished by means of the ancient pyramids was this myth transmitted from generation to generation.*

We must stop looking at history as Western history, Eastern history, Japanese history, or American or British history. The 19th-century history books by Tenshin Okakura and even those by the famous French historian Jules Michelet (1798—1874) and others created a false consciousness in people that the center of Asia was empty. By neglecting Central Asia, the European West and the Far East cannot meet each other now as they once did so gloriously in the past.

In the 21st century, we should look at our Earth with the eyes of a satellite. From up there, there are no national boundaries. Eurasia that floats on this blue planet is connected with Africa, and the wide desert belt of Sahel traverses from North Africa and continues through the Near and Middle East straight to the Gobi Desert. While we are gazing at a satellite photograph of this brown belt, we begin to see where *roads* were.

Part IV. Civilization and the Natural Environment

Letter 17

On the Banks of the Indus

Dear Friend,

I have here a clay seal. The image of a rhinoceros is engraved on this seal, a piece of one-inch-square unglazed pottery. Its four pictographic characters in the Harappan language remain undeciphered.[84] This seal is one of the things excavated at Mohenjodaro on the Indus River. On this seal are hidden 5,000 years of history.

The Indus civilization existed along the banks of the Indus River that flows through the central part of present-day Pakistan, and extended from the southern province of Sind northward to Kashmir and the nearby Punjab region, then west to the historic Baluchistan region and into Iran and the coastal area of the Persian Gulf. Furthermore, it stretched southeast to the Gujarat[85] region of India and the Bay of Canbay. All this defines the vast range of a single civilization. Its size in those ancient days surpassed that of the civilizations of the Nile and Mesopotamia combined. A new theory is emerging that the Indus civilization may not only have been the largest but also the most ancient in origin of these civilizations. The high degree of sophistication of this civilization has only been known since 1921.

Concerning this oldest world civilization, we have not yet learned even one hundredth of what we need to know about it. The ruins that are thought to belong to this same civilization number about one thousand, and the excavation sites dealing with it are no more than ten.

---

[84] The Harrapan language contained 250 to 500 characters.
[85] Gujarat is the name of a historic region. Ahmedabad is a major city and former capital of the modern state.

These include Harappa, Mohenjodaro, and Kot Diji. Moreover, the
excavation work on each of these is only 10% finished.

Even though it's still a mysterious civilization, information about
the excavations at Mohenjodaro has astonished the world since 1922.
The 35,000 relics unearthed from this area have already told us many
things. The list of things found includes designs that will remind those
familiar with Japanese history of the Jōmon period (prior to 200 B.C.)
and of the gigantic jars in what looks like the colors of the Yayoi style
(200 B.C.-250 A.D.).   And we have lingams as well as women's
accessories, and many lovable clay figures, mainly toy animals.   In
Japanese these figures are described as *kosetsu. Kosetsu* means inferior
in technique but tasteful because old-fashioned and simple. In addition
to the rhinoceros mentioned above, there are elephants, wild oxen,
antelope and goddess figures.   These are represented in the
multitudinous incised seals. They tell us of the existence of a people
who lived an agricultural life and enshrined the goddess of bountiful
harvests.   Moreover, they carried on commercial activity using the
Indus River.

There is one important statue of a priest-king who is thought to have
had both sacerdotal and governmental powers. With the exception of
that statue, all the clay figures of the human body are female as seen in
the original form of the goddess Shiva. There is also a bronze statue of
a dancing girl, but hardly any bronze tools have been discovered.
These statues and toys are uniformly small.   While visiting the
museums of Karachi and Mohenjodaro and viewing the small clay
figures that disseminate the meaning of life in their unique way, I
noticed a great contrast.   These figures, which are from one to a
maximum of eight inches tall (3—20 centimeters), are strangely
incongruous with the huge jars adjacent to them. The jars are twice the
size of something our arms can reach around.

§

To reach the site of these artifacts, I am flying north from Karachi in
a Pakistani prop plane. After about an hour, at last the color green
begins more and more to show up in the brown desert beneath my eyes,
and here and there an arc-shaped lake comes into view. Each of these
lakes is water left over from a change of course by the meandering
Indus.   Mohenjodaro occupies a place where the vast plain rises
somewhat.   Even as I was standing among these ruins of brick

buildings, a gust of wind arose; soon I saw a tornado going through. It rolled up great sheets of sand dust from the plain.

Friend, you may want to ask me, "What is there to see in Mohenjodaro?" In that place there are no Egyptian temples, no giant statues of pharaohs, no Greek columns, no Babylonian castle walls, and none of the sculptured reliefs of Persepolis. What Mohenjodaro has are only heaps on heaps of bricks. In the highest place, there is a partly collapsed dome-like structure, but it is thought to be a 2nd-century A.D. stupa[86] of about the time of King Kanishka; in other words, it is something that has no relationship to the original Mohenjodaro. When Buddhists came from Gandara in the north to this land in the second century, they probably found a brick city that was not too different from what we see now. For it had ceased to exist some 1,500 years before their time.

As I've already intimated, Mohenjodaro has no shrines and nothing we can call a palace, nor does it even have a tomb. The only human bones so far discovered are those of the fifty people who may have been killed at the end of the Indus period when the Aryan invasion of the region occurred. If we say Mohenjodaro had no impressive architecture, then what on earth is the value of these ruins for the history of civilization? Surprisingly, the answer is *city planning*. Someone has characterized Mohenjodaro as like Manhattan, and there is surely a sense of modernity in the avenues and streets intersecting at right angles and in the houses lined up in an orderly row. Moreover, in almost every house there is a private well. Certainly there is a sewer drain, and covered sewers run under the streets. The city then was a prototype of modern waste disposal. So it can be said that, Mohenjodaro contained a very early example of a complex and efficient municipal sewer system.

Even in London in the Elizabethan era of the 16th century, a time of extreme prosperity, sewage was running down the middle of the streets in ditches. A full-scale sewer system was constructed in Paris only in the 19th century with the public works of the urban planner Baron Georges Haussmann (1809—1891). Of course, in 19th-century Japan,

---

[86] A stupa is a mound of bricks or earth used for burials and adopted in Buddhism for relics of Buddha and his main followers. In Burma and beyond, it became the pagoda. *A Dictionary of Non-Christian Religions* by Geoffrey Parrinder (Philadelphia: The Westminster Press, 1971).

such a thing as sewage disposal did not exist—except in the rivers. Nevertheless, at least 4,500 years earlier, the citizens of Mohenjodaro were all enjoying an advanced sewer system. 2,500 years before Rome, they had large public baths.

Just as in Harappa, which was 370 miles from Mohenjodaro, the western fortress area was separated from the eastern residential area. In the residences built for 40,000 people, all of the houses were almost the same size with the same floor plan. Coupled with this fact is the lack of palaces for authorities to live in. These findings show the existence of a democratic society that had a kind of equality and was therefore a society for the citizens themselves. Actually, as we examine the faces of these clay dolls, we see good humor reflected there. You may fall under the powerful illusion that you are seeing something like Romanesque statuary. It's as though we can hear the healthy laughter of the people whose countenances have been engraved.

What were people doing to sustain life? All evidence points to this city as a great commercial center surrounded by the fertile plain of the Indus River. According to what I am told, the products accumulated and distributed here included grain, as well as cotton, spices, and porcelain. And in those days, a lot of these things were shipped down the Indus River to the ocean and thus to cities lying along the coast. The discovery of seals with old Harappan writing in all these places proves that the trade routes lay along the coasts of Magan (Oman) and Bahrain on the opposite shore of the Arabian Sea and from there ran overland to various sites in Mesopotamia. These records of commercial activity have also been unearthed to the south, in the coastal regions of India.

Studies of the Indus civilization are still in their infancy. In the early twenties when scholars were treating "Indus culture"[87] as a part of "Sumerian culture," it was assumed that trade was by overland routes. However, this theory is now no longer held, and another explanation has come to be widely accepted that there were early, frequently used sea routes. I saw one diagram that gives proof of the sea-route theory. It was drawn by Professor Rafique Mughal, a Pakistani archaeological authority. While the ruins of the early Indus civilization (4,000—2,500

---

[87] The name "Indus Civilization" came later. A beautifully illustrated *National Geographic* article for June 2000 (Vol. 197, No. 6, pp. 108-131) confirms Dr. Hattori's main data and hypotheses, while summarizing ongoing findings and the riddles that keep surfacing. Many competing theories are set forth.

B.C.) were concentrated along the Indus River, during its mature period (2,500—1,750) it extended to the coasts of Iran and India. After this, what is called the late Indus civilization (1,700—1,200) arrived with its decline and decay.

Looking at these developments in this way, we can discover the leading role of the sea in the interchange among civilizations even in the remote ages of antiquity. When I consider this, it is opportune to say a word about the tribe called Mohana, a small number of people who live in modern Pakistan. These people are said to be the only survivors from the tribe who created the Indus civilization, and even now they float on the Indus in special boats. It is reported that every year before the period of flooding, they select a site on the Indus River which directly faces Mohenjodaro. There they perform festive rituals that are believed to have special significance. In recent times, people spell Mohenjodaro as Moenjodaro. The idea behind the name Moen is thought to be, "Hill of the Dead" (in the Sind language, *moen* = the dead). If we associate the name with the present scenery that is desolate and dreary, the word hits the mark. But it is hardly believable that the original inhabitants would so name their own city. The most reasonable way of thinking about this must be to presume that Mohenjodaro is a variant of Hill of the Mohana.

§

However, my friend, an unexpected crisis has attacked this rare heritage that awakened in the 20th century from the sleep of remote antiquity. It is the damage from *salt*. If you undertook to walk across Mohenjodaro today, you wouldn't be prepared for the 120° F (45° C) temperature. From spring to fall it is that hot in the shade. Moreover, since there is no shade, if you've forgotten your hat you'll surely succumb on the spot to sunstroke. Luckily for me, I went there during the winter. Nevertheless, at every location in the ruins, servers were carrying trays and offering us cups of cold water.

Touring on foot, we notice the fact that the city's brick walls are becoming pure white in their lower parts. When I touch and taste the white area it is saline caused by a residue of crystallized salt. This happens when the underground water is sucked up on account of the intense heat and, due to capillary action, there is both osmosis and evaporation in the bricks. Then salt remains there. And this salt causes the bricks to disintegrate. Buildings that have lost their foundations must collapse.

The government of Pakistan has taken note of this dire situation and, with the cooperation of UNESCO, has commenced special repairs for the sake of preservation. First, they harden the foundation of the houses with cement. The cement is also used to prevent moisture from rising into the walls from the foundation. Next, they dig scores of wells in the area around the ruins; then they let the water that they have pumped from the wells flow in the drainage ditch they have built as a ring around the ruins, and, finally, they let it all flow back into the Indus River. Because of these measures, the water table that in the summer had risen to within two yards of the surface of the ground gradually began to go down. However, in order to keep Mohenjodaro from further disintegration, fifty-six wells would be necessary. The total budget needed to cover the cost of this construction was to be $16,000,000, and international cooperation was needed to complete this project.[88]

§

Friend, ruins are humanity's memory. There is an extreme irony in the fact that once the revival of this memory by means of excavation has begun, at that very moment salt conspires to destroy it. However, since there is a blank in part of humanity's memory if we don't excavate, our duty is to conscientiously preserve the part of the city being excavated.

One point must be considered about this salt damage. There is no trace of such a phenomenon during the time when Mohenjodaro was prospering, and, in fact, this is a recent threat. It is surmised that there are various causes such as changes in the course of the Indus, weather modifications, and desertification of the surrounding areas, but it is likely that this phenomenon was precipitated sixty years ago when the Sukkur dam was constructed about 30 miles upstream from Mohenjodaro! From the point of the dam, the canal from which water is drawn for irrigation has a higher water level than the Indus. The most reliable theory seems to be that the leakage of water from the irrigation canals raises the water table. This situation reminds us of the environmental pollution associated with the Aswan dam in Egypt.

---

[88] It was finished in 1997.

It was because the Aswan dam would submerge the sites of many ruins in the area of Nubia, including the Abu Simbel Temple, that UNESCO in 1960 initiated its first international campaign for the preservation of cultural heritage. The new concept of "the cultural heritage of humanity" was born at this time. However, as an effect of dam construction, the salt damage along the coast of the Nile is indescribably bad. The artificial stoppage of water that ought to flow defies nature, and we must realize that Mother Nature will exact retribution for such defiance.

Nevertheless, preservation has brought about an unexpected harvest. In Nubia many international teams of archeologists were dispatched who discovered from ten to twenty previously unknown ruins, and it is reported that these discoveries have contributed to the progress of Egyptology. In the case of Mohenjodaro, during the digging of the aforementioned watering wells, the diggers uncovered several ancient ruins 58 feet deep. In 1964 English archeologists drilled down 39 feet and did not discover these ruins.

From the digs associated with the recent well drillings have come items closely related to the Indus civilization: pieces of porcelain, bracelets, charcoal, bricks, etc. Such discoveries prepare us to adopt a more precise view about the first founding of Mohenjodaro. We may safely conclude that the establishment of Mohenjodaro occurred 1,500 years before the previously estimated date of 2,500 B.C. This means that Mohenjodaro was founded, not in 2,500 as usually claimed, but in 4,000 B.C. or about 6,000 years ago, and is thus the oldest known city.

§

Friend, if we are standing near that vast river, the Indus, we can see a simple farmer here and there. An oxcart pulled by two beasts is passing along piled up with a mountain-like load. The scene has not changed at all from what we see embodied in the terra cotta toys from ancient Mohenjodaro. When Alexander viewed the great river after going through the Khyber Pass, this is what he saw. And the same thing was seen by the Buddhist King Kanishka at the time he reached the mouth of the Indus. When I consider this fact, I feel that a period of a thousand years is concentrated in a moment.

The Hill of Mohana (known to us as Mohenjodaro) does not tell us its story. That story may be contained in the Harappan hieroglyphics left to us. But because of the absence of long documents and the lack of parallel data with other languages, as on the Rosetta Stone, the decipherment of this language is not yet possible. Even the analysis based on the use of computers in Finland has not yet broken the code. However, I got a strange feeling that this picture writing is similar to the original form of some Chinese characters. It is also said that the cuneiform (wedge-shaped) writing created by the Sumerians is an improvement on picture writing, but what is the source for the picture writing itself? Many questions such as these come to mind.

Quite recently a Belgian scholar made an astonishing disclosure. It concerns the points of agreement between the *rongo-rongo* writing of Easter Island (which has its own riddles of civilization) and the hieroglyphics of the Indus civilization. When we look at a table of comparisons, we easily see at least twenty characters from the two scripts that have identical shapes. These ancient hieroglyphs for the human form, domestic animals, houses, and the sun and moon, make short work of the thought that these depictions are purely accidental coincidences. But the argument of this scholar goes on to state that there is, indeed, a common origin for human civilization in the Indus area and that from there civilization spread gradually on an East-West axis by land and sea routes.

A researcher of menhirs (megalithic monuments) in France states that the origin of the culture of these prehistoric stone monuments spread *westward from* the Middle East to the Mediterranean and Britain, and *to the east* as far as Indochina and Japan. "The ecological view of the history of civilizations" by Tadao Umesao also shows basically the same pattern in the movement of civilizations east and west from the central part of the Eurasian land mass, but it lacks the maritime point of view.

Recent scientist-adventurers are paying careful attention to the role played by the oceans. The Ra, Kon-Tiki and Sohar were ships taking part in modern experimental expeditions concerning sea routes. The Sohar was a replica of an Arabian ship from around the 9th century A.D. In it sailed a young Englishman who confirmed that a sea route existed from Oman to China. So the *sea* was deep in the heart of this young man and the other people in these expeditions which confirmed the sea as the main artery of cultural interchange.

Five thousand years ago, the seal of Mohenjodaro was carried to far-away countries from the Indus region by ships. At that time the waters of the Indus were already connected with all the waters of the world.

Letter 18

Death of a Lake

Friend,

In my previous letter, I spoke of the Indus civilization. I stood on the "Hill of the Mohana People" (Mohenjodaro) where 5,000 years of history were concentrated. At that time I had the question in my mind, "How was a city belonging to such a great civilization born, and how did it happen to perish?"

I have not felt at all satisfied with the theory that the city became extinct because of the attack of the Aryan people in 1,200 B.C. What's more, now that's no longer believed in the scholarly world. The Aryans were not horse riding people like the Mongols and Scythians. If they had attacked, they would have occupied and used the cities of the Indus civilization. But there is no evidence that they did this. In addition, the period when we know the Aryan people went southward is not exactly the same one in which Mohenjodaro collapsed. The bones, the discovery of which I mentioned in the previous letter, are seen as belonging to a mixed group of about fifty people, but that is too small a number to indicate a large massacre. And, since no other bones at all have been found, the idea of a general massacre is an improbable solution.

I am sure that the ruin of these cities is due to changes in the climate and environment.

If they had the intense heat approaching that of today, who would choose to locate a capital in such an area? It would be irrational. Therefore, it was not like that. The land 6,000 years ago must have had a mild climate and fields of grain. The crops could be transported on the Indus River. So it is thought that the harvests were carried to this city of Mohenjodaro and that commerce with neighboring countries prospered. The forms of many animals that inhabited this area at that

period are incised on *seals*. It is only logical to believe that when the
temperature rose and the land became dry and barren, little by little the
people left.

I would like to call attention to some special wells of Mohenjodaro
as evidence for this. The innumerable wells we can now see look like
thick chimneys. The sun-baked bricks of Mohenjodaro had two
standard sizes—which tells us of a system of mass production dating
from the early period of the Indus civilization. And people must have
stacked the bricks especially carefully for the wells that were to be the
sustenance of their lives. The floors of the dwellings were surely
aligned with the top of the wells. As the detritus of the centuries built
up, it was necessary to extend the well tops upward to the floors of the
new houses. So the wells became deeper and deeper or taller and taller
as we see them today. The buildings of that later age have nearly all
collapsed and disappeared, leaving only the extremely sturdy wells.
Here we can clearly see that the later construction was coarse compared
to the earlier construction in the Golden Age of Mohenjodaro, and that
all this suggests economic decline due to an environment that was
changing for the worse.

The level of Mohenjodaro
in its late period must
have been near the top of
the well shaft that now
looks like a chimney.

§

Friend, the primary factor in the fall of the great civilization of Mohenjodaro seems to have been a climate change. Should we consider this change to be caused by the general warming of the earth that ended the glacial period? And should we consider also the change in the flow of the Indus? Such thinking first appeared as a solution suggested by the physical geographers. However, I think that the primary factor, at least locally, was human activity, that is to say, deforestation. As was the case with many other cities of antiquity, Mohenjodaro also was built and rebuilt through the centuries at several levels. Moreover, the builders had no rocks but only bricks. The baking of the bricks necessary for such construction involved an enormous amount of deforestation. The felling of so many trees and shrubs changed the climate and that in turn brought about the rise and fall of cities. Recently, this has become the conclusive word on the subject.

Shall I give an example? Ephesus of Ionia (Persian at that time, Turkish now), which was an ancient Greek city, had a great shrine and amphitheater. It is the birthplace of the philosopher Heraclitus, whom Socrates respected. Its death is now understood to be due neither to foreign enemies nor to the retreat of the Mediterranean coastline, but to the cutting down of trees. A more familiar example of climatic change concerns the extreme desertification in an east-west band of the Sahel region across Africa with the Sahara Desert on the north. This began with the immigration of European people. It is now thought that the cattle raising they brought in destroyed the delicate ecosystem and that the desert wiped out the verdure. I remember one time that tears came to my eyes while viewing a documentary film showing cows that had only foliage to eat and had become so thin their bones stuck out. The similarly thin African people were chopping down the few trees that remained in the desert to feed their cattle. This land was so parched that it was cracked and broken. I understand those people's short-range drive for survival in cutting down the last trees. But by eating the leaves of one tree a cow could survive only a single day. And the replacement with a comparable tree will take thirty years.

It has also been said that the construction of the Great Wall of China across thousands of miles turned the surrounding land into desert. Only quite recently have people recognized that *the greatest means of water storage and conservation on earth is the roots of living trees and shrubs.* In ancient and medieval times, not to speak of the modern era, human beings did not have the idea of planting trees as a means of maintaining their water resources.

§

But, my friend, I doubt that you think the lack of trees is the only danger to the environment due to human ignorance. Right now in Central Asia a lake is about to die. It is the Aral Sea.

This huge lake with its 250 mile diameter is worthy of being called a sea. Once it proudly supplied 10% of the former Soviet Union's caviar and a fish-catch of 40,000—50,000 metric tons annually. During a 30-year period its water level has declined two or three feet each year. Now it has sustained a 40% loss of its area and a 60% loss of its water volume. What was once the bottom of a wide body of water is now a huge desert. There the iron hulks of abandoned fishing vessels can be seen. Fish no longer live in the lake that is continuing to dry up. Since the salt content is very high, only six kinds of sea life, including shrimp and rays, still manage to survive. If this trend continues, by the year 2010 this "dead sea" will become nothing more than just a white trace of the former Aral Sea. But there is a strange fact. Nineteen miles south of the present Aral lake shore in a little village in the middle of a salty desert there is a fish cannery where 900 people are working. They transport fish from the distant Caspian Sea to the town that formerly was on the Aral Sea shore. The plan was to attain again the same high number of fish that were reportedly caught by the Caspian Sea fishermen in the former Soviet Union when each community was required to report its production quantity to the Central Committee. At that time the Caspian fishermen reported their number while the same number was reported by the Aral Sea factory, thus doubling the official count. Now we can see the traces left by this desperate people who must have (in Churchill's phrase) shed blood, sweat, and tears trying to build canals fast enough to keep up with their receding lakes so that they could once again launch fishing boats and reach their impossible quotas of fish catches.

Even well water in the whole area embracing the three newly independent countries of Kazakhstan, Uzbekistan, and Turkmenistan, contains an admixture of so much salt and agricultural chemicals that it is really not fit to drink. However, the people living in this area must drink this water. Therefore, deformity in children is a common occurrence. 80% of all babies are born prematurely, and their rate of

mortality has doubled. Actually, 90% of mothers and children suffer
from anemia. In certain areas, the stunting of children's bodies has set
in. Three million residents have been affected by the continuing crisis.
Why did such a situation arise?

In antiquity the Kyzylkum (Qyzylkum) Desert in this region
contained one of the Silk Roads of the steppe, and it was a place where
nomads roamed. In the first part of the 1960s, the central government
of the Soviet Union decided to set up a large-scale cotton farm in this
desert. Rice and melons were also planted, but the main effort
amounted to a cotton monoculture. Based on this impractical decision
by Moscow, the production of cotton trebled from six million acres in
1960 to eighteen million acres in 1987. At first it was praised as "white
gold" and quickly developed into an export industry. However, to
achieve this kind of production requires water. The government
irrigated the huge farming operation with water from two rivers, the
Syr Darya and Amu Darya, which fed into the Aral Sea.

A huge investment was made in chemical fertilizers to go along
with these extensive irrigation projects. Now the two rivers can only
pour a thin stream of muddy water into the lake. And the quality of the
important crop of cotton went down from year to year so that now
nobody is buying it. But girls still pick the cotton. They have nothing
else to do in a single crop agricultural economy.

§

Furthermore, there is an almost unknown cause. I think that what I
must mention now is a serious example of the megalomania of the
former Soviet Union.

In Turkmenistan there is the vast Karakum desert adjacent to Iran,
but the government in Moscow got the bright idea of building a great
canal, the Karakum Canal,[89] all the way to the Caspian Sea from the big
Amu Darya River. They planned to make this desert green. This idea
was not completely arbitrary because the Amu Darya has sometimes
changed its course in history, and one time it even emptied into the
Caspian Sea. Therefore, the natives called this a "crazy river." At any
rate, the fantastic plan was actually to build an artificial river something
like the Seine stretching 850 miles (about the distance between New

---

[89] Also, on some maps, designated as the Karakumskil Kanal.

Fishing boat hulks on the salty desert that was once part of the Aral Sea

© 2000 LAEL PORTER

York City and Atlanta, Georgia). When this canal opened, it was widely touted as a "triumph of science and socialism."

However, the project flopped because when water flowed through the canal it stopped short of the Caspian Sea. The reason is that, since the builders pushed the canal through the desert using engineering methods equivalent to simple ditch digging, the flow of water was sucked up by the sand, as well as evaporated by the hot air of summer. Therefore, the water completely vanished before reaching the Caspian.

From the vicinity of Mary (or Merv) I went sailing on this Karakum Canal, and I also saw it from the air, but from both vantage points the scene unfolded as I had imagined it would. As in the instances of the Indus and Nile valleys, here, as far as the eye could reach, it had become a region damaged by salt. The precious water of the Amu Darya River is here literally evaporating due to human arrogance and folly.

In 1992 at Rio de Janeiro a summit meeting was held under UN auspices to consider "The Earth and Development." The desertification of the earth ought by now to be impressed on every mind as a man-made calamity. As the basis for this calamity I see the classical mechanistic science embraced by Western Civilization in the 17th century. It's a way of thinking that says, "Nature ought to be conquered and ruled." Hasn't the moment indeed come when we should earnestly reconsider such ways of thinking? Mother Nature does not like surgical operations on herself. If medical treatment is required, let it be a kind of homeopathy—as used in some vaccines. Above all, let it be administered gently.

The example of the Aral Sea is one of development carried to the extreme of exploitation and even ruin. It's an example of the destruction of nature in that area and also of human life for those living there, and even of development itself. This environmental problem ought not to be treated only by external analysis from the natural sciences but also from a social science approach. That means taking into account the needs of both people and nature and their mutual interdependence. Such a relationship is called symbiosis in biology.

Letter 19

The Garden of Eden in Africa

Friend,

I have seen the Garden of Eden.

It happened when I visited the vast Selous wildlife reserve 250 miles south of Dar es Salaam, the capital of Tanzania. That was the summer of 1988 when I came to Dar es Salaam to open an exhibition jointly held by UNESCO and the government of Tanzania. As my daughter Yurika and I flew from Nairobi, there came into view the superbly beautiful summit of Mount Kilimanjaro covered with its perpetual snows. This sight caused me to remember Hemingway's mention of the carcass of a leopard found atop this mountain. Since the leopard does not live at this height, why did he climb so high?[90]

I was thinking that I would like by all means to take this opportunity to see the wild animals. The wildlife preserves at the foot of Kilimanjaro, on the Serengeti Plain, and at Ngorongoro crater, have been designated a world heritage. However, the number of small buses on sightseeing safaris coming to these national parks from capitalist Kenya exceeds the number of elephants in some places, and the same rhinoceros is the subject of thousands of photographs. I was told that if I wanted to see the wildlife depicted by Hemingway, I had to go to Selous. That would be the farthest animal reserve from Kenya. Even from Dar es Salaam we must be prepared to endure a rough road for ten hours.

While we were worrying about finding a means of transportation, an unexpected solution turned up. The Pakistani ambassador saw Yurika

---

[90] Ernest Hemingway, *The Snows of Kilimanjaro and other stories* (New York: Charles Scribner's Sons, 1927), p. 3.

at the ceremony for the opening of the UNESCO exhibit and invited us to visit him at his residence; as soon as he heard that we wanted to go to Selous, he provided us with a light plane for the trip.

The Cessna aircraft finally loaded the three of us, one of us even in the seat next to the pilot. It flew for about an hour over the savanna, and when the pilot found a break in the clouds, landed on a strip that had been cleared of trees and shrubs. Of the many airports I have seen, this one was the most extreme in its lack of facilities. It was barely an airport. It didn't have a hut or a tent or any people. While we were wondering what to do next, a jeep from the nearby safari camp came to greet us. We were taken to the camp with the eggs and other daily necessities that had been loaded under our airplane seats.

The camp's reception desk was a circular counter surrounding a baobab tree. After we took a little walk, we discovered about ten tents among the trees, but on that day the only other lodgers were an American married couple. The astonishing fact is that each tent was furnished with a flush toilet and shower. I recall hearing how a young German woman, the manager of a light aircraft taxi service does not drink the water in Dar es Salaam but does drink the water in Selous. In contrast to such civilized amenities, if we take a step outside, we can see the tracks of a large herd of elephants that just recently passed by and so we have to climb the baobab tree when the elephants show up. For that, a ladder has been set up.

The baobab tree is the symbol of Africa. When five grown people link hands, they can only just reach around its trunk. The tree looks unbalanced because its short branches grow from its huge trunk like the feelers of the sea anemone. Very wisely this tree drops its leaves in the dry season, in this way preventing evaporation of moisture. Then it patiently waits for the rainy season.

§

After conversing with the director of the camp, we decided to go out on a boat safari in the evening and a motorboat safari in the early morning of the next day.

As we were going downstream by small boat before sunset, we found the water had been dyed a beautiful silver. From our boat we saw buffalo and zebras feeding on grass at the riverbank, green alligators that swiftly slithered into the water, and hippopotamuses by the hundreds. Each of the hippopotamus families has its territory. In the evening the hippos go up on the land where they munch the grass;

at dawn they return to the river. The routes they take are used over and over, and the banks where they climb about a yard up from the river to the meadow tend to collapse. Often the banks are so steep that I think they have to heave their massive bodies almost vertically out of the water, and when they've climbed the bank one of their savanna pathways awaits them. It's a "hippopotamus walk."

However, the lead actors of our safari boat entertainment are the birds. Countless multi-colored birds are dwelling at the water's edge, in shrubbery, and in the rock cliffs. Pretty birds are making nests in the hundreds of holes in the cliffs. Eagles are staying in coconut palms that have lost their tops in floods, and kingfishers are beautifully demonstrating their fishing skills before our very eyes. It is said that Europeans and Americans especially like to come here to bird-watch.

The next morning while it is still dark, we start to penetrate the boundlessness of nature. In our special safari jeep, the guide is armed with a gun loaded with real cartridges. Sitting next to the driver, the guide keeps a sharp lookout. No animals feel safe in such a wildlife reserve because hunters are here on safari. When the animals sense the presence of people, they run away at full speed. But our guide, by carefully judging the wind direction, has managed skillfully to take us toward some animals. He sees animals invisible to our eyes. He whispers, "Simba!" (lion), and points to a clump of trees. Nothing is visible to me, but by looking extremely carefully through my most extended zoom camera lens, a lion family appears hiding in the shadow of a tree and waiting for its prey.

What constituted a really grand sight was the spectacle of hundreds of zebras and gnu all intermingled in rows at a watering place. Also at another place, I was taking snap shots surrounded by the giraffes and antelopes, when suddenly we caught sight of a great flock of pelicans flying in from every direction. The pelicans began to rotate just as in a circle dance, and when all had come together, they flew down to the river in an orderly fashion.

However, what I most vividly recall is a lake surrounded by beautiful verdure. All around the lakeside are many birds and animals standing in the brilliant light from the morning sun. Numberless species of birds and animals are living together in harmony like one big family. I had never before experienced the virginal pureness of mother earth to this degree.

"Ah, this, indeed, is the Garden of Eden!" I felt this with deep emotion.

§

My friend, this paradise is rapidly disappearing. One major factor is the increase in the human population and, along with that, is the increase in consumption. Because of economic development and exploitation, within a hundred-year period 55% of the rain forests have been destroyed. It is frightful that about 50 plant and animal species disappear from our planet every day.

Poaching is the greatest enemy of the large land animals that we want to preserve. At the end of World War II there were 2,500,000 African elephants. That number has now shrunk to 500,000. Moreover, yearly about 80,000 more are said to be killed by poaching. There used to be 25,000 black rhinos, but now there are only a scanty 3,000. So, if things continue as they are now, in the 21st century both kinds of animals will become extinct.

Now the authorities of Kenya and Tanzania have set about taking firm action regarding the poachers. No longer do they just arrest them; they shoot them to death on the spot. When I went to the camp at Selous in the summer of 1988, I heard that already in just the first half of that year the teams of rangers had shot 54 poachers. Furthermore, Kenya's president in 1989 had shown his determination to stop poaching by having at least twelve tons of confiscated ivory burned in the presence of journalists.

However, poaching did not decline. The reason is that one rhino horn brought a price greater than the local people's wages during a two-year period. Furthermore, when Kenya's official announcement of the abolition of ivory hunting was made in 1975, it had the opposite effect from the one hoped for. Accompanying the sudden jump in price, there came increasing skillfulness on the part of the crime networks. Gangs of well-armed poachers, at the risk of their lives, crept in even from neighboring countries and began a war on the teams of rangers patrolling the regional nature preserves and the international parks. The young rangers die for a monthly salary of less than $20.

§

Friend, by what means may we solve this problem? The only solution is to get rid of the demand for tusks and horns. Already several Arab countries have stopped using as a status symbol the crescent sword handles made of rhino horns. But the horns are still sold in Southeast Asia, not as aphrodisiacs as people say, but as a specific remedy for fever. At a meeting in Lausanne in 1991 several nations agreed to ban the import or export of ivory, but five African nations did not sign this pact. In Zimbabwe the reason given publicly for the slaughter of elephant herds was that they injured agriculture; this rationalization included baby elephants. Elephant skins coming to America and ivory going to Japan all pass through Hong Kong and Singapore. In fact, 40% of the ivory of the world is said to be used for the ivory chops (name seals) in Japan.[91]

The image of an elephant family on the savanna probably does not occur to the mind of a customer buying a chop at a store counter. However, we should think of the direct implication for the life or death of our inheritance from nature: "This earth has no substitute." We need to keep this in mind as we carry on our ordinary activities such as the daily use of a Freon spray can that is helping to destroy the ozone layer of the atmosphere, or the casually splitting apart of our wooden chopsticks thus depleting the world's forests. Will we human beings sooner or later be living on an earth lonely and desolate because it has no more elephants or rhinos but only cement dust settling on the flowers? Another question is, does this one earth belong only to human beings? Animals do not have words. But if they could speak, they would insist that there are not just "human rights" but also the "rights of other living things." I think the time when they should have their say is coming—indeed, has already come.

The Japanese people who since the Meiji Restoration have run after the Great Powers as they cried out "Development! Progress!" now may look back to the aborigines. Shouldn't they learn from the Ainu? The Ainu are a people who live with nature in a gentle way, having discovered the communication of the soul with nature. Human beings are not the only ones granted life; both the deer and the bear which humans eat also have to worry about what to eat. For the Ainu there are no ceremonies other than those related to *life*. The Marimo (or Iomante) Festival at Akan Lake gets its name from *marimo*, a ball-like water weed found solely in Akan Lake. Unfortunately, it has become a new ceremony fashioned to suit the tourist business; it is not the

---

[91] In 1999, the Washington Convention that banned the export of ivory made an exceptional quota for Japan.

original ceremony.   In contrast, the authentic bear-sacrifice festival, also called "Iomante," is a bear "sending back" in the sense that the soul of the bear, which has helped sustain human life, is sent back to heaven. It returns to paradise by means of the arrow shot powerfully into the sky. The ceremony expresses gratitude for all of the mercies of Mother Nature. The *kamuisomi* (the Ainu name for the sprinkling of saki on the earth in an offering to nature) has the same kind of origin as the ceremony performed by the Siberian hunter Dersu Uzala in the great film by Akira Kurosawa.[92] There are similarities to this even in the ceremonies of the various Indians of South America. Indeed, in all these ceremonies the value and importance of all living things are acted out. I feel in these a true philosophy of symbiosis or living together. Since the 19th century, what is called "animism" has suffered diminished credibility as a way of thinking.   However, mature reasoning may give animism more credence in the coming age.

§

In Tanzania they distinguish even the hours in a different way. Seven a.m. for us is one for them; in other words, it is one hour after sunrise, and the next hour is two, and so on. I remember Senegal's tom-tom drums also mimicking the passage of time during the day. It begins in the stillness and tranquillity of dawn. The drum gradually receives a harder beat and faster rhythm reaching its peak at noon as it speaks of the joy of life; then, in early afternoon, it becomes almost listless and lazy, tapering off till it vanishes with the silence of evening. There seems to be chiseled into the daily routine of working under the sun an intertwining of the life of many animals and many people—an ongoing "tree of life" which has not yet become extinct.

---

[92] The reference here is to the international prize-winning film *Dersu Uzala the Hunter*. In the film the hunter-guide warns the soldiers on his explorer friend's expedition, "If you shoot all the beasts, we'll go hungry."

Postscript

My Friend,

As I am winding up this correspondence, my mind flies back to the hill of Delphi thirty years ago. It was the season of Easter. As a student at the Sorbonne, I had joined a Greek excursion planned by the *Cité Universitaire de Paris*.

Three Japanese students, in order to see the sunrise, left the village while it was still very quiet and climbed the white lane. The sun that showed its form between two mountains shone directly upon Apollo's shrine on the hill. It's the shrine where Socrates received the message from the oracle. The sky was blue as blue could be. Whenever we happened to look at the roadside, we could see the flowers sparkling in the spring sunlight. The shade under the leaves was not even black; it was as though the shadows were tinged with purple.

As we overlooked the sea from the top, the valley below was tinted a smoky white. The valley indeed was covered by olive trees with their powdery-white leaves. I thought it was as though these things—that sea of olive foliage, the shrine to sun god Apollo, the stadium, and the amphitheater—all symbolized the birth of humanity

I have heard someone say, "Culture is a matter of *cut and clear* in order to cultivate the land." Nature in the Mediterranean area, if we exclude the abundant sunshine, is not at all gentle. It is filled with rocks and stones, and is dry and severe. Human beings have plowed it up and planted olives there. That has become the basis for getting food and housing. If people hadn't done this, probably *culture* in its higher sense could not have been born. Culture is born where there is *scholé*, which in Greek means "the leisure used in learning" (hence, the word "school").

While looking up at the pillars of Delphi, which stand erect against a dark blue sky, I was seized by an emotion which caused me to realize: *This is a declaration of humanity. It is against nature. . . . In that sense, Greek pillars may all be called "human pillars"*— caryatids.

In the Delphi Museum, along with the famous bronze statue of a charioteer is the stone called Omphalos, "Gaia's navel" or the center of the earth. In this museum, I came to understand how the *stillness* of Egypt, which coexists with the gods, changes into the *motion* of human beings. Also, the birth of a *human consciousness* that seeks the center of the world in mythology seems to me to be in synchronicity with the *declaration of humanity*. In Greek mythology Zeus has chosen Delphi as the center of the world and the dwelling place of Apollo. The viewpoint of the gods is shifting to the human viewpoint. In Egypt, Mesopotamia, and the Indus Valley, as well as in Judaism, the gods see the humans. In Greece, humans *see* gods. There the gods become more and more human. Whenever you go to Greece you can see the transition in the Delphi Museum. Before your eyes, the gods are becoming *infinitely* human.

§

Three times we climbed to the Athenian acropolis. One time was when the west was dyed red by the sun as it sank into the Sea of Salamis; another time was in the simply dazzling morning, when the gable of the Parthenon was just cutting the bright blue sky; and the last was in the deep of night. Only during the three nights of a full moon was the Acropolis unilluminated by electricity. Takashi Harada, and Kōichirō Shinoda, and I, all of us on French government scholarships for foreign students, climbed the Acropolis by this moonlight. When we sat down on the marble ledge surrounding the shrine of the Parthenon, the moonlight shone blue bringing the marble architecture into bold relief with the lights of Athens spreading beneath us. That scene evoked a question from someone, "Why are ruins so beautiful?" Time was flowing like a quiet stream. Harada, as a scientist, said, "It is settled that the time of construction is the most beautiful time. If that were not so, the architect-builder would not have built in that way. Therefore, we ought to say that even crumbling ruins are still beautiful." However, there was something in me that called out, "That is not so! We are just captivated by the ruins themselves as they are now. There is beauty that is different from an art form. What can that be?" The bluish pillars of the Parthenon stood out boldly in the full moon, and suddenly an answer to that last question revealed itself to my mind:

There is a "beauty of time." Ruins are crumbling. However, in them lies concealed the time of antiquity. The memories of the joys and sorrows of the living people who constructed those ancient works are locked up in them. When we stand before the ruins, that all appears in an instant. That kind of emotion is what creates the beauty of ruins.

In one building or one stone we feel a disclosure of the vastness of human history so that we have the feeling that we are but a drop in the great river of life. That night on the hill of the Acropolis was a beautiful moment, a moment that even resembled God's grace.

The expert on French literature, Takeo Kuwahara, once spoke of the "dignity of the Earth." In order for human beings to shape a human future, there must be a moment of gazing at the past. I think he means that there must be encounters with human memory and that we must protect cultural assets for the sake of that memory.

INDEX

This index consists of important subjects and proper names excluding only the Chinese dynastic names that occur throughout the book. Where standard spellings exist, they are used in this index.

About the Author and Translator

Eiji Hattori is a professor at Reitaku University near Tokyo. He holds doctorates from Kyoto University and the Sorbonne (University of Paris). Dr. Hattori served UNESCO for 21 years as senior information officer, director of cultural events, and coordinator of the "Integral Study of the Silkroads—Roads of Dialogue," project He is a council member of the International Society for the Comparative Study of Civilizations (ISCSC) and a board member of three other societies.

His publications include: *Thinking at the Crossroads of Civilizations"* (Kodansha, 1995), *Man, Science and Nature* (Edition du Mail, co-author, France, 1994), *Science and Culture: A Common Path for the Future* (Reitaku University Press, 1999), *Paysage of Encounter* (Reitaku University Press, 1999), and twenty-five articles on culture and comparative civilizations.

Dr. Hattori is multilingual with fluency in Japanese, French and English. His use of English was crucial in the production of this volume. The Hattoris have residences in Paris and Tokyo.

Wallace Gray has most recently been visiting professor at Kitakyushu University in Japan. He is Kirk Chair of Philosophy and Religion Emeritus at Southwestern College in Kansas. His Ph.D. is from Vanderbilt University. He is currently an ISCSC council member.

His publications include: *New Keys to East West Philosophy*, co-authored with John Plott (Asian Research Service, Hong Kong, 1979), *Global History of Philosophy* IV (1984) and V (1989) co-authored with John Plott and Michael Dolin (Motilal Banarsidass, Delhi), and numerous journal articles.

The Grays make their home in Kansas.